In The House Of Me

ISBN:
Hard Cover 979-8-9879890-3-6
Soft Cover 979-8-9879890-4-3

Book Cover and Illustration by Malialani Dullanty
First edition 2023

This book is dedicated to the women who have served as a portal to self-reclamation, three specifically whom share a variation of name:

Melissa Febos offered me the language of empty consent which had previously been absent inside my healing journey. Through her writing, she offered a directive to turn the lights on inside *the house of me,* for which I'm profoundly grateful.

A second Melissa demonstrated for me how, when a woman betrays herself, she will undoubtedly and inevitably betray the boundaries of other women. I hope she has since turned the lights on inside herself in whatever rooms she was previously unwilling to go into.

Me. The other 'Mel'.

I am a woman who has reckoned with and saved her own story by taking and leaving what she needed to unlearn and reclaim from both Melissas.

I am a woman unapologetically *for* myself.

Contents

IN THE HOUSE OF ME

A path from self-abandonment towards self-reclamation
through a practice of embodied consent

Mel Gentry Bosna, MSW, LCSW

With Illustrations by Malialani Dullanty

A gentle consideration as you begin:

This book explores content your body may or may not be in a season to explore, process, witness or repair yet—if so, please know that's okay–it's more important to honor where you're currently at than steamroll ahead. If you notice your body feeling fatigued or activated by the material, I hope you pause and return only when you're ready to, please take care of you.

The book is written by a licensed clinical social worker who is in private practice, it is intended to be a resource for those who read it. However, it is *not a substitution for professional therapy* or any other type of support best suited for your individual needs and vulnerabilities. Each reader is encouraged to practice curiosity towards their body's cues, emotions, needs, capacity and overall readiness for exploration.

Topics include religious trauma, sexual violence, white supremacy and personal accountability. Continue as it feels in alignment or shelf this book at any point if it no longer honors you to continue reading.

May you find and utilize safe people who witness your story and healing as you journey through the tender milestones of both, may you always find your way back home to yourself.

Key Terms

The following key terms are defined by personal use and interpretation. The terminology is neither comprehensive nor absolute in definition, however meant as a guide for the specific content and application of this book.

Activated/Triggered, *adjective*
The body's response to real or perceived threat as experienced through shifts in breathing, heart rate, muscle tension, focus or presence. May also be marked by feelings of overwhelm, powerlessness, paralysis or dissociation.

Bodies of Culture, *adjective*
A description I learned from trauma therapist and somatic abolitionist, Resmaa Manakem, which is used in place of the descriptor 'people of color'. He writes, *"I speak of bodies of culture to refer to all human bodies not considered white.... This both acknowledges our existence as human bodies and displaces the other terms that make white bodies into the norm and otherize everyone else."* (R. Menakam, 2023)

Boundary, *noun*
The separation of self from others in order to honor limits, delineate ownership and increase safety. Boundaries are internal and relational in practice and often the expression of consent.

Consent, *noun / verb*
This book explores connection to our inner *'yes, no and maybe'* and the nuanced expression that subsequently follows, ranging from a spectrum of empty to embodied consent.

1

Key Terms

Culture, *noun*

The use of culture here specifically refers to default/mainstream beliefs, customs and practices broadly shared by people in the United States, which are internalized individually and upheld collectively. Group dynamics and power either uphold rape culture or work to dismantle it, consent culture cannot develop without a separate foundation.

Dissociation, *noun*

A protective stress response of disconnection from the self, body or present moment with the sole intention to survive what the body is experiencing and/or interpreting.

Embodiment / Embodied, *noun*

The experience of being connected to one's body; feeling attuned to one's needs, emotions, power and limits in the present moment.

Gaslighting, *noun*

Manipulation through dismissal and discreditation of a person or groups' experience with the intention to invalidate and/or avoid reality and responsibility. This can be practiced with others as well as internally within yourself.

Harm / Moral Injury, *noun*

Injury caused regardless of intention that subsequently hurts another person and also betrays one's own value system and integrity.

Home, *noun*

The place where body, self and spirit experience increased presence and safety allowing for alignment without fear of judgment, harm or exile. Home becomes the foundation for authentic expression.

Homebodied, *verb*

An embodiment practice which affords us access to our inner compass and internal world and therefore allows us to be at home with ourselves more fully.

Integrity, *noun*

Consistently being the person you claim to be, acting in alignment with the values and commitments you profess in a way that builds and maintains trust. When behavior becomes discrepant, a person with integrity actively practices humility, ownership of error and initiates repair, prioritizing realignment over emotional comfort or reputation.

Nervous System, *noun*
One of several bodily systems that interprets both the world around us and the world inside us, with specificity to threat or danger whether perceived or real. The nervous system activates the body as a protective, survival measure and when overly responsive, may disconnect us from other supportive parts such as our intuition and executive functioning.

Non-Binary Thinking / Non-Duality, *adjective*
The creative possibility of more than two opposing beliefs or expressions to exist as valid possibilities, allowing for a broader spectrum of choice and collaboration. Instead of things being black *or* white, all *or* nothing, good *or* bad, non-duality allows for an expansive bridge of shades and liminal space between.

Patriarchy, *noun*
A system that simultaneously gives cisgender men structural power over others while simultaneously robbing everyone (including men) of their full humanity. Patriarchal power systems harm all people and genders alike through discrediting and diminishing individual dignity, restricting emotional capacity and exploiting the human body.

Religious Fundamentalism, *noun*
Strict adherence to a set of religious beliefs or texts which subsequently prohibit individual human interpretation, application and agency. Fundamentalism in all expressions attempts to enforce beliefs onto others regardless if they ascribe to the same values, positioning itself as an absolute truth. Fundamentalism appears easily threatened and therefore seeks to govern the bodies, beliefs and behaviors of others to protect its narrative, fragility and power.

Reparative Accountability, *verb*
Intentional ownership and follow-through specifically in places one has caused harm regardless of intention. Mature repair is an aligned action motivated from compassion and integrity rather than obligation and fear. It centers the experience, needs and emotions of the person who has experienced the most harm and/or holds less structural power. Reparative accountability sees the risk of avoiding ownership as greater than the risks involved with being seen as a person who caused harm.

Key Terms

Self-Abandonment / Self-Betrayal, *verb*
Impulse and behavior resulting in making yourself small, betraying your intuition, needs, boundaries and values in order to avoid or 'resolve' conflict and therefore reduce anticipated abandonment from others. Abandonment therefore occurs internally before experienced relationally. This is commonly referred to as people-pleasing.

Stress / Trauma Response, *noun*
Biological, evolutionary reactions that aid in survival when either real or perceived threat occurs and the body becomes activated. Stress responses are individualized based on environmental data and each individual body's split-second interpretation of safety. This book explores five common stress/trauma responses which are commonly referred to as fight, flight, freeze, flock and fawn.

Third-Way Practice, *noun*
An alternative approach which rejects the duality of only having two polarized directions, identities or options to align with. Rather than being reduced to being either good or bad, right or wrong, progressive or conservative, third-way embodiment allows for curiosity, intuition and self-governance to practice one's values outside of a binary framework.

Trauma, *noun*
Any experience the body interprets and stores as activating rather than releasing and resetting to safety. This occurs regardless of how we or others think experience and memory should be weighted–how the body remembers eclipses what the brain may try, even successfully, to forget.

White Body Supremacy / Whiteness, *noun*
An intentional, strategic system created and maintained by white people, on behalf of white people, which centers white bodies and culture as the default experience and in such a way as to provide an illusion of invisibility to those who benefit from it while oppressing bodies of culture. White body supremacy is embedded in every United States institution and perpetually denies the full humanity and dignity of bodies of culture, people of color and white people themselves. It harms all involved.

Key Terms

"White-body supremacy—and all the claims, accusations, excuses, and dodges that surround it—are a trauma response. This response lives not inside psyches, but deep within bodies. The attitudes, convictions, and beliefs of white-body supremacy are reflexive cognitive side effects, like the belief of a claustrophobe that the walls are closing in. These ideas have been reinforced through institutions as practice, procedures, and standards". (R. Menakam, 2018)

Foreword

Standing around the island in Mel's kitchen that summer night, a collection of friends from her respective spaces gather. Some of us already familiar, some of us complete strangers, all of us trusting the safety we've become accustomed to from our common friend. The desert evening light pours in through her windows as we pass plates, share tapas and fill crystal glasses with bubbly drinks. We warm to each other with ease, scraping the bottom of bowls, reaching for last bites without apology. No appetite too big. No laughter too loud. No occasion needed. Gathering for the sake of being *with* each other. I've driven across town that evening simply because Mel offered, *I'd really love for you to be here if it feels good for you.* Well, that and knowing Mel is in the final stages of her research on the path of consent for this book and will be inviting us into a bit of her process.

Gourmet pizza arrives and Mel tosses a gorgeous salad. We pile our plates with good food to fill our good bodies as the sun begins to set, move into the dining room to find seats at her table beneath soft overhead lamplight. Fresh flowers and dietary choices tell us she's been expecting us, that she's made preparations for our individual needs. She's gone before us, curating an evening with care. Mel's open door and long table set with intention frames our feasting on seconds and thirds, our storytelling and our belly-laughing. Pizza sauce collects at the corners of our mouths and we let melted cheese string long from our lips. I refill my glass and sit back filled full on more than the warm dough and fresh greens. The last light hits just right with desert dust particles shimmering overhead, the safety around this table feels like magic-making.

A smirk peels across my face realizing Mel is doing exactly what she does so well, right here in her own home with her own people: she's making room.

The flow of energy around the dining table shifts as we digest our dinner and conversations. Mel invites us to move into the living room. Matches spark and a cluster of candles are lit on the coffee table surrounded by pillows on the floor, blankets draped over chairs, enough room for each of us and an invitation to listen and respond with as much or as little as we feel comfortable to share. She sets the tone with questions from her research and our circle then weaves its own path processing through trauma, TikToks and everything in between. Mel holds that space wide open knowing everything belongs. Every story told. Every memory held. The candles burn down low as one by one we check the time and slowly begin to unfurl from our chosen nooks. Each of us free to leave when we need to, welcome to stay longer if we'd like, the flow changes once again.

A few of us stay and move out back to sit around Mel's fire pit. The current of connection keeps us lingering for a few more minutes of this magic. Around the fire is where, once the shadows grow long, we often discover even deeper stories within ourselves or allow for even sweeter silence between each other. Flames lick the night sky glittered with invitations to feel microscopic AND to expand deep and wide into our bigness. Mel already communicates her own boundaries which allows us the freedom to spread out in ease and take up space within them. Finally I say my goodbyes and head out into the night to find my way home.

In The House Of Me is a brilliant work on consent, breaking new ground right before our very eyes, but you will see that for yourself with every sentence you underline and every paragraph that steals your breath. What may surprise you is how Mel moves us through the flow and depth of her work the same way she moved the flow of a gathering through a shared meal and shared stories through her home—room to room, gently and with so much safety and care.

Every component of Mel's research is collected, metabolized and shared from her deep well of professional expertise woven together with her personal lived experience. Every word on these pages comes from her own full-bodied practice of consent going ahead along the path and making more and more room. You may sense the weight of these sacred spaces she has prepared for us to navigate as she asks deeper questions, owning more of herself and her own story to light the way. You may also feel the heat of the fierce flame burning deep in her belly on behalf of the humanity, dignity and pure magic of every. single. person.

Mel guides us through, arguably, some of the deepest waters. She allows space for us to confront our own reflections with honesty and calls us into greater integrity while showing us ways she practices doing so herself, lighting each room gently and on purpose, room by room in the house of *herself*. She is in relentless pursuit of safety for the most vulnerable and marginalized and has given us language to recognize spaces needing care with ourselves. You may find yourself and your own stories between these pages, striking a match and illuminating room by room the house of *you*.

This new language, this conversation surrounding consent, is (to use Mel's word) terraforming: enhancing the capacity for an environment to sustain life. Her work is creating new safe ground for us to stand upon and while busting up old ground, long since parched and cracked by harmful systems designed to preserve themselves. Her research is validating as well as convicting, hopeful as well as uncomfortable, but her care for us through every story and every idea is unmatched. The pages you hold are a cosmic invitation for us to explore this new ground.

As I read the last page I was surprised by the tears spilling from my eyes. Exhaling long and loud and still catching my breath I whispered to myself:

We are safer for this work.
We are worthy of this work.
And we are not alone.
Mel has gathered us on this path of consent.
New ground forming under our feet with every step.
Mel has given us the gift of this blueprint.
We give ourselves and each other the gift of turning on the lights.
Just enough to see by.
Just enough to find our way home.

–Corinne Shark, author *Slow Burn*

Author's Invitation

Recently a friend came over for dinner on a rare Monday night when my family happened to be out of town. We swapped stories about what's disrupted us recently along with ways we've been practicing honoring our intuition, practicing accountability and having hard conversations with people in our lives. We ate strawberries and salmon and toasted our growth. I threw the ball for the puppy and pulled a bridge from the tarot deck she'd brought with her. She read my cards, watching my face as I silently processed what each card read and she eventually said what many others have echoed throughout my life: "Perhaps someday you'll tell me more about why trust feels so hard."

I smiled at her comment, shrugged, knowing it would be easier to name if it were a singular break instead of how it actually exists: it's grainy, less like the foundation moved by the earth's quake, more like infinite particles of blown sand that hover in the air, each eventually settling into the cracks of a shortened childhood, nearly invisible to the eye yet existing all the same.

Trust has been a tender thing for me, at least in part because no one taught me consent. Not knowing who or how to trust nor understanding the practices of consent and boundaries resulted in a few decades spent guarding what I assumed others would diminish if I ever let my guard down, all while feeling misunderstood for how fiercely protective I was of myself.

Gaslighting is a tactic of discreditation, a practice of sowing doubt into the bodies and stories of people harmed. In addition to experiencing gaslighting from those with something to gain from our confusion, it often presents as an internalized option many of us practice within ourselves. It's easier to minimize the grains of loss we cannot see rather than name and confront them, less risky to point to the foundation the house was built upon as seemingly sturdy than to explore at what point it became uninhabitable. Acknowledging how parts of us have perhaps left before our physical bodies had the same option can be an untethering process we're not always ready for.

I've gaslit myself out of habit, mostly through the misremembering of my own story–how often have I defaulted to another's narration of a memory rather than recall that I too was there, I know enough. While I haven't trusted others easily I have learned overtime to trust the source within me. I am learning to risk more relationally in direct proportion to the grains of memory and parts of myself I'm making mountains out of, the wonder of being a soft and sturdy ground of being. My trauma is no one thing of mistrust and neither is my healing.

I am both my home and also her homecoming. I believe this about you too.

Why this book, why now, why me? I'd be remiss to start writing without answering this question. It'd be easy to throw in the identities I hold and perhaps what qualifies me as a voice on consent–therapist, researcher, woman, survivor, parent–each of these contribute to why consent matters to me and I'm guessing you share some of these same identities which is why you've chosen to pick up this book.

If I'm honest I'm writing this now because the practices of consent have more often than not been absent from my life. *I needed this book* and while the last few years have produced a growing body of work on consent, nothing yet has offered what I needed during the times I felt powerless, confused and outright harmed about what was happening to me, be it a random Tuesday afternoon conversation with a colleague or the paralysis of harassment at a bus station.

The language of consent is evolving, although a vast majority of Americans associate it exclusively with sex. While consent *is* a foundational practice of sexual ethics, reducing it to sex alone leaves many people uncertain how to navigate other situations where it need be applied. For example, while writing this chapter I had a memory surface from a previous season of my life when I was a professional photographer. I had documented a wedding in December and afterward, while walking to my car, found myself followed out by the groom's spiritual mentor who had officiated the wedding. He peppered me with personal questions as I walked away from the venue, telling me how he'd *noticed* me throughout the day. I didn't want to be noticed let alone cornered into this conversation.

In The House Of Me

I stood outside in the dark, laden with all my photography gear, assessing how to exit the conversation while still feeling obligated to answer his questions despite having no other connection to him. I was physically exhausted from having been on my feet all day and wary from having had a multitude of other experiences throughout my life with being noticed by spiritual men. I was weary knowing I had a long drive home still to come with babies waiting for me there to care for. I was spent and empty before I later became afraid and angry.

To this day I don't remember how the conversation progressed except to say I'm certain a point occurred where I no longer felt present in my body. By the time he asked "*if anyone had ever hurt me and if he could pray for me*", it's likely my head nodded 'yes' while every other part of me meant no. His left hand stretched to my shoulder, he audibly prayed and I stood there blended with a quiet child-part of me, who waited, watching for the opportunity to leave. With his left hand still on my shoulder, he finished praying and his right hand intentionally landed hard on my chest hitting it with a loud thud. He blew on my face, locked eyes with me, waited for a response I couldn't give him. I did what so many of us do in situations we want to end and found myself thanking him so I could get away.

The scene replayed for the thirty minute drive home, it felt disconcerting yet also familiar. I cycled through an internal gaslighting loop, mad at myself for 'letting him' corner me into conversation, for allowing his hands and prayers to cross my boundaries. I felt I knew better because I had grown up surrounded by men like him. It wasn't until later while unpacking my gear and processing the wedding day's events with my partner that my body synced hearing his appalled reaction, physically shaking in rhythm with my partner's voice, "*Wait–WHAT–he hit your chest?!*"

I hadn't wanted what happened to happen and yet shamed myself for it nonetheless. Worse things had happened to me before and I felt I ought to have known better. I had said yes to parts of it while meaning no, parts happened without my permission all together. I was not present within myself when things began to feel unsafe and my body responded how many of our bodies do when early on in life distressing things happen and there is seemingly no way out of them, which is to say, parts of me disappeared and made themselves small.

I left me–we always leave ourselves when it feels like our safest option.

Mel Gentry Bosna

Like many of us I grew up in an environment where autonomy wasn't valued. What developed from this lack was a duality of fierce determination to self-govern while still living out frequent self-abandonment, I often felt conflicted. I couldn't practice consent because hell if I could even define it *let alone* access my internal world to know what I was willingly consenting to. I now understand this as a trauma response.

I believe the tension between these parts was in fact the catalyst for why I pursued clinical social work as a career. I worked alongside pregnant women who were incarcerated for drug possession and use, adolescents who sought to disappear through starvation as a way of regulation, teens who'd been trafficked across the country, dehumanized and exploited. I couldn't name yet what I wanted to see healed until years later when I started holding the outcomes of trauma with more curiosity and subsequently started my own healing work.

What I want for my clients is rooted in the same desire I have for all of us: to feel safe enough to belong and exist as we are.

Consent is the bedrock of safety.

I'm writing this book now as it remains culturally relevant, there's an urgency with offering these stories and the subsequent tools I've learned to as many people as possible. The world of survivors is steadily unleashing a rebelliousness that does not just hope but *intends greater safety*; many of us have the taste of consent on our lips and we're hungry for more.

As a clinician I remind my clients that building trust takes time and practice depending on how the people we're experimenting with respond when we risk opening up. I don't presume vulnerability nor readiness before my clients are both willing *and* ready to practice with me, nor do I expect to be given trust without proving I won't exploit them or run from hearing what needs to be named. I am no one's healer but my own, rather I see myself as a mirror, reflecting back the truth and goodness that already exists within them, also, within you.

I don't presume to have your trust either so here's what you can expect if you continue reading: this book contains parts of my story, reflections on client stories as well as several dozen others who voluntarily participated in a national qualitative research study on how people access internal consent and practice it

14

with others. Explored are ways consent development gets hijacked along with paths you might try with reclaiming more of yourself. The hope is for readers to depart with tools to experience a fuller, resonant consent while also feeling seen and validated through the shared stories of others. This is a book about how to know your inner '*yes, no, and maybe*' and further develop self-trust which often leads the way with consent and boundaries.

Throughout you'll read excerpts from conversations I had in both professional and personal spaces. Identifying details were changed to increase the anonymity for those I spoke with and the pronouns used honor the identity of each person whose story is shared. I'd ask you to witness with openness their stories and relate them back to your own when you have the bandwidth to do so, explore the implications of what was offered alongside the outcomes that resulted.

Like many others in 2017 I found myself sharing two little words in a social media post: Me Too.

Tarana Burke, activist, author and community organizer founded the #MeToo movement in 2006 which she details in *UnBound*, a profoundly moving memoir which explores her childhood and adolescence, personal trauma and healing journey and the social movement that's taken root as a result of it all.

#MeToo has furthered the development and our understanding of the social constructs of consent culture and the ways systems of oppression at large, and patriarchy specifically erode it. To borrow a familiar metaphor, trying to change culture without dismantling systems of power is the equivalent of trying to build a house upon sand. Power-over models will never yield power willingly which is why vulnerable communities experience ongoing harm. Burke's work is ground-breaking, world-altering, and I will continue to see the #MeToo movement and the social reckoning that's followed it with her energizing leadership at the helm.

As a clinician who specializes in Complex PTSD and chronic childhood sexual trauma, it isn't uncommon to hear stories of boundary violations and violence inside my office, however with the 2016 American presidential election of Donald Trump and 2017 judicial hearings of Brett Kavanaugh I experienced a shift from some to suddenly most my clients sharing stories of harm. Clients who had previously sought out therapy for other reasons were triggered by what was happening socially and politically, so much so our conversations pivoted and therapy goals were reprioritized. The season sifted for me what's been missing from mainstream conversations about consent.

Consent is largely still defined by the letter of the law–the need for this is purposeful, often enough a black/white definition is absolutely necessary in order to define criminal behavior and pursue legal accountability. However the actual practice of consent is *significantly* more nuanced and complex. To date, there aren't enough of us practicing robust consent let alone enough of the public yet aware of the many layers to it. In the last decade since I started gathering resources on consent, boundaries and embodiment, I went from finding hardly anything available to a growing body of resources to refer to, yet haven't read the book I most needed when I myself was in crisis.

In order to practice consent, we need two specific things: first to be embodied enough to access our internal world, and secondly, to feel safe enough to express it in the outside world once we know our inner lines and intuition. The outcome of not feeling embodied nor safe enough leads to self-abandonment, betrayal and empty consent practices.

The short-answer to this question, 'why this book, why now, why me' is this: I want a safer world for more of us to exist in as our full selves. For this to happen, we must return home to ourselves, specifically to our bodies which in turn allows for deeper integration of the parts of our stories we haven't previously felt safe enough to be with and heal. This involves settling urges towards self-abandonment and internal gaslighting that surface as protective measures to secure attachment. Additionally, we must discern who is safe enough to be in a relationship with and *how to stay with ourselves* despite living in a world hell-bent on our ongoing self-departure.

May we do this together, may you feel my presence in your corner.

Mel

Part I: A House Abandoned

"Abandoned houses seldom turn out to be as empty as they appear."

–Robert Dunbar

Chapter One

HOUSES WE LEAVE

I grew up in a small community in Phoenix, Arizona, the United States' 5th largest city. Despite the city's size my world itself felt small. We lived on a noisy street, my parents drove a distance to take me to school and otherwise I stayed mostly inside. There seemed to be a consistent presence of fear although I'm still discerning if it was theirs or mine–that's the thing about being a child, one often absorbs the feelings and beliefs of those around you.

In his book *The Body Keeps the Score*, Bessel van der Kolk describes various methodologies and approaches with treating childhood trauma, exploring how important the relationship is between children and caregivers. Essentially, what the parent or caregiver cannot emotionally hold and be with, the child cannot process. Throughout this book I'll be sharing both personal experience alongside my professional perspective regarding how an unsettled body and nervous system disconnect us from parts of ourselves.

Many people who consistently feel dysregulated, overwhelmed or anxious before the age of twenty-five have greater difficulty discerning between their intuition and their anxiety due to how both the human brain and attachment styles develop. I'll share more about why and how this happens later on but for now, note the experience of being dysregulated and how the symptoms of anxiety and trauma are not choices children and adolescents are making–I'd argue they're not experiences or symptoms *any* humans would choose for themselves.

What parents cannot feel or offer support towards, children undoubtedly will struggle to express. A parent cannot help a child co-regulate when they themselves don't have access to their own emotions or the corresponding skills needed to regulate them. So whether the origin of the fear was mine or my parents, we felt it. This translated to regularly peering out the windows, pulling down the blinds and rechecking the locks. I chronically felt like I was being watched and to date, all my nightmares take place in the house I grew up in.

Additionally, the energy of our community seemed centered around church and the cowboy culture of the wild west. I grew up the daughter of parents devoted to Christian ministry, which subsequently led them to employment by a church. My parents lived, breathed and served the gospel which means the majority of my childhood memories involve these practices too. I don't know that my parents cared *how* I was involved in church as long as I was involved, it was always a family affair.

Prior to evangelical ministry, my father worked in construction and to this day my mother cleans houses to make ends meet–they remain willing to serve their community and I've always admired them for it despite how our beliefs differ about god and the world.

I was the first person on either side of my family to attend college, none of which any of us navigated smoothly. My parents seemed proud of me although honestly would've likely been content if I hadn't pursued a career as long as I was happy. Growing up in a predominantly white, conservative church meant I wasn't presented with many options if I wanted to fit into this community. Later on I share how religious systems impact consent development, family systems as well.

For now I'll shine a spotlight on how, when we're not taught to trust our bodies and intuition, we look to people and processes outside of ourselves to tell us what and who is safe. Dr. Hillary McBride affirms this when she writes, "*It is very hard to leave systems that have harmed us by teaching us to ignore and mistrust the signals in our bodies indicating we are being harmed*", meaning the more disconnected from our core we are, the more consistently we'll engage in self-abandoning practices.

Common default options for my community included being straight, cisgender, abstinent until marriage, married and monogamous for life. I remember my shock at 20 when I discovered a good friend had voted for Al Gore in the 2001 presidential election–up until that point it hadn't occurred to me a person could identify as both a Christian *and* a Democrat, which is of course laughable now yet highlights the rigidity of the binary framework I grew up with.

I found myself in situations where a lack of options started posing more of a threat than the situations themselves. The first time I took a pregnancy test was when I was twenty-one and with a man I didn't want to date let alone co-parent with—I remember standing terrified in that little bathroom waiting for the results, feeling trapped with seemingly nowhere else to go but to another powerless corner. Options matter, without them there's nothing to practice consent with.

The religion I grew up in emphasized free will as the reason for harm's existence in the world, however as I started pulling on the threads of that ideology the dissonance felt was profound–I couldn't reconcile free will if there was no other option *but* god or the hell he created. This was one of many unraveling seasons of my early adulthood—looking back I experienced it as a disruption in my spirituality however I can now see that it was related to my hunger for consent. If I was going to choose a god, I wanted that choice to come from a conscious surrender and not from a fear of eternal torture. I couldn't name it then but realize my longing for a consensual world was already bigger than my need for absolution.

Much of this remained intellectual instead of embodied however, meaning that while I knew I had options I'm unable to say whether I could access them emotionally. This is a common observation I have in my office too—my clients often come in with an awareness of what they want to change, or hell, what they *should* be doing differently, however continue to find themselves reenacting old stories, participating in familiar patterns, defaulting to the parts of self that feel accessible despite the conflict with what they know or believe to be true. New ground often feels shaky, we ache for it yet have parts guarding us from taking it.

Mel Gentry Bosna

This liminal space between what we know and feel may lead to more internal exiling and shame, over time creating an internal disruption large enough for options to present themselves whether we access them from choice or crisis. I encountered it in a painful season in my own marriage when I explored parts of myself afraid to leave, afraid of being left and also afraid to stay in the marriage I was in. I put every option I could think of on the table—I'd always *known* I could get a divorce however it wasn't until that season I experienced how limited I actually felt in exploring it.

Through practices we'll explore later in the book, leaving became a necessary option I began to feel and access as a choice, just as staying married did. The paths available traveled from my thought processes down into intuitive decision making. I could discern what was in alignment with my integrity and what I want for my life. I was able to know, feel and own a way forward, not from what I *should* do nor from what my fear wanted to rescue me from, but from a true source of self-trust.

In addition to staying or leaving my marriage, I freely presented myself other options too: opening my marriage to polyamory, ethical non-monogamy, exploration of queerness/queer relationships, practicing singleness by choice, never partnering again, exploring asexuality, demisexuality, conscious celibacy, witchcraft, becoming a Buddhist, hard-core mystical nun–you name it and it's likely I considered it! I put every option thinkable on the table, sifting through each with curiosity, noticing the spaciousness and restriction inside my body, practiced naming them with a full mouth, looked at myself through each lens, stared straight as I could at myself in the mirrors my trustworthy friends and therapist reflected back for me to see.

I took my time, inviting each option to have as equitable a chance as possible and to my surprise, discovered that at least in this season of my life, I wanted monogamy and I wanted it with my partner. This might not seem all that noteworthy to someone who grows up with permission to choose for themselves what's in alignment with their desires and values—however it felt terraforming for me. It was the first time in my life I was actually *choosing monogamy* with him since previously there were zero alternative options due to the beliefs I was raised with and how they were stored in my body.

The outcome looked the same on the surface, no one would've known it's change otherwise, however the energy of the decision's underbelly was radically different. I chose monogamy inside a heterosexual relationship at thirty-nine-years-old, at which point I'd already been married for over fifteen years.

It was both healing and also unsettling—I began wondering how many other people were actually consenting to the relationships they were in, or, if like me, they hadn't been presented with alternative options to choose from. Thus began quantitative research on the relationship between consent and monogamy which evolved more broadly into a qualitative research study on consent, self-trust and safety. I became more invested in how people access and practice consent and *all* its implications and layers, sexuality and coupling being only one of them.

I'd posit now what I'd previously practiced was compartmentalized consent at best, empty consent more often than not—parts of me had chosen marriage, chosen my partner, chosen monogamy, however other parts of me hadn't because I wasn't able yet to even access them. In the next chapters I define different ways we define and practice consent.

We can only listen to an inner wisdom once we've welcomed it home–we can't welcome it home if the cost of doing so will disrupt the house we've constructed within the broader community we're living in. I hadn't felt connected to myself nor safe enough with those around me to explore a different path. No one had modeled one as an alternative without fear of disapproval, ostracization or shame attached to it.

Options matter.

Without them we cannot choose what's in alignment, without embodiment we are restricting consent, without relational safety we are not as present nor empowered as others would have us believe. I gave myself permission to change the dynamic of my marriage fifteen years in, however it came with significant disruption. While I would do it again on behalf of the energetic outcome it produced, I don't want to minimize how initially disorienting the experience was with finding a way back to myself.

For a season I lost my appetite, power, voice and my boundaries as I wrestled with what I wanted, who I wanted to be and what was at stake with reclaiming it. It ultimately brought me more fully home to myself however the process was not initiated from internal safety. I've engaged intentionally with healing practices surrounding that season, to this day I remember the way my body trembled during particular conversations I had with my partner while redefining our relationship and before either of us felt safe and in alignment with the options we had. My body remembers acutely how fragile and uncertain the space between us felt–I wish that for no one.

I offer this as it feels important you understand some of where I'm coming from: I know the cost of having limited options, I experienced the relational and social risks involved with self-alignment, I can recall how it felt to cry myself awake in the shower, refusing to settle for a lesser life while embracing a new, shaky foundation. The disruptive experience of following your inner compass, advocating on behalf of a life worth living and setting the necessary mother-loving boundaries to support it will undoubtedly bring you to your knees before it elevates you to an inner throne.

Stay the course, you are not alone.

Chapter Two

SAY MORE

The research participants were a group diverse from one another with regards to upbringing, gender identity, race, sexuality, education, age and religion. I formally asked the participants the same twelve questions with additional, individualized questions threaded throughout the interviews based on what they shared. The questions can be found in the appendix of this book as reflective journal prompts or a discussion guide for a book club.

The interview questions were explored with research participants, clients, followers on social media, holiday family dinners, people next to me on airplanes, birthday parties, doctor office waiting rooms and the volleyball sidelines at the local YMCA–essentially anyone willing to talk with me. Admittedly I could've sat with a giant bowl of popcorn and continued with these conversations for the remainder of this decade, I thoroughly *loved* talking to people and hearing their life experiences surrounding topics of consent, boundaries and self-trust.

One of the early questions in the interviews asks what we remember learning about consent and how the definition has evolved into whatever it is today. The answers to this specific question ranged from furrowed brows, blank stares and often outright laughter, "*Ha! What? Nothing, absolutely nothing! I learned zero things about consent*" was the overall summary of the replies I was given.

What often trailed after those responses though was a drop-off into silence, an awkward pause as the reality of what had been missing in childhood settled into the cracks of their experiences. For some, it was the first time they were admitting to someone the impact that being denied personal sovereignty has had on them. For others it appeared to be the first time they considered how they'd never been taught anything about consent at all. I watched with compassion as some participants uncomfortably came to terms with the fact they *still* weren't sure of consent's definition.

My office has a 9ft x 6ft window, right above the $14 table I sourced at Goodwill, the one with chunky legs and zero drawers but that's tall enough for both my chair and therapy puppy to fit under. I've noticed people seem drawn to look in one or two places in the office when vulnerable emotions or fragmented memories surface. If they feel safe and connected enough they'll look at me and hold my gaze, however it's more common for their eyes to fixate on the floor or travel leftward over to the window.

The ceilings are tall and every few months or so I flirt heavily with the idea of hanging curtains, the extravagant over-the-top kind, something with velvet or tassels or better yet, a circus brocade that I would love but would maybe be off-putting to someone else. That's as far as I usually get with exploring the idea, mostly because the window is where our eyes inevitably drift when we go searching for responses to hard questions or when we face within ourselves a thread of memory emerging to be named. I do it too—often when I'm gathering my own thoughts regarding what to reflect back in conversation, I'll find my eyes drift to the light streaming in.

On the other side of the window is a steep grassed hedge that slopes quickly into a parking lot. There's a small bush with white and yellow flowers that blooms half the year, the birds love it most when it's flowering, however even when it's not in bloom there are always one or two birds that come and bop their little bods around on the branches and windowsill. If it's not the birds that draw our eyes over it's the large sky above REI which neighbors the hidden parking lot between our buildings. The sky is often cloudless and bright as most Arizona skies tend to be, however on the days a monsoon's clouds roll up I pull the blinds all the way to the ceiling, letting the room fill with a different kind of light and energy. My clients' eyes often tear, synchronizing with the sky's downpour, reminding me how crying in the company of someone who cares about us is one way we release a heavy thing we've been carrying.

I repeat myself often in client sessions and research interviews—how it's important to honor the limits around the timing and readiness of what we're disclosing. It's not uncommon to feel willing to share but realize as we're doing so there's a part of us that isn't yet ready for the experience of what comes along with disclosure. Have you noticed this before? How something can feel fine-fine-fine and then suddenly overwhelming, panicky? What's often happening when we go from feeling fine to activated is that our body is cuing us into a need for safety, it's perceiving a threat, whether a current threat or one stored in our body from a previous experience.

Our nervous system responds by providing this data through activation, while parts of us can intellectually talk about an experience and know it is in the past, the way it's often stored in our memories and bodies may have us still feeling threatened therefore making it difficult to discern between what happened to us previously and what's happening now. That part deserves our attention, a pause, reassurance, maybe a bigger break. Our body is a wise guardian and intends our safety. Depending on how we experienced harm we may experience things as safe in situations that feel familiar to our body—we may also interpret things as unsafe because they feel unfamiliar to our body. I frequently invite my clients to explore if the reasons they're reacting to something is because it's unsafe or unfamiliar as they're important distinctions. Either way, we practice curiosity and pay attention to our bodies.

This is counter-practice to how I was formally trained as a clinician which was more or less to 'gas' trauma work–rip the band aid off, pull someone in and their truth out regardless if they trust you or feel ready to share it. We see it modeled in journalism and court rooms too, this push for information when people are in a vulnerable state. The over-exposure of our stories doesn't heal us in the same way that trying to forget what happened isn't enough to heal us either. The therapeutic goal isn't desensitization, it's integration. We want our bodies and minds to reset to safety.

Mel Gentry Bosna

I now refuse to engage in relationships the way I was trained, especially of the therapeutic kind. I'm invested in the process of *how* we get somewhere more than where we actually end up. This means that conversations (including those occurring in therapy offices)take time, and that overall people end up feeling safe and valued as we honor the pace they feel ready for. This is one of the many ways I engage in a consent practice, following both internal as well as relational limit cues.

There's a fluidity and energy to the exchange, a necessary retraction at times. I often pause conversations to ask how someone's body is feeling, whether they need a break or want to pivot to another topic. More recently I've stopped conversations mid-sentence when I observe someone's nervous system as activated, discerning they are about to share what perhaps a part of them feels desperate to get off their chest while also seemingly experiencing an inner conflict about what they're about to reveal.

I now gently interrupt, have people pause, take a few breaths, ground in the space we're in and practice curiosity around the parts of them that seem to be withholding consent, the parts that are in distress, still unready to share. I remind them how I'm less invested in hearing a confession–I am no one's priest–the goal is safe connection, trusting when things feel safe enough inside they'll feel safe enough with me. As a result, the distress often dissipates and they are more fully able to name their pain with less risk of self-abandonment or another person's rejection.

In addition to the words 'me too', which provide many of us comforting validation, I find myself saying another phrase when a person practices sharing their story—two little words meant to communicate curiosity: *Say more.*

The following conversation took place with a research participant weeks before Christmas. Ollie and I had been talking about their family system and how it felt to be a child growing up in a home that was intolerant of anything 'different' than the default model of how to be human (specifically in their case: straight, cis gender, Hispanic and Catholic.

They shift their body on the couch, breaking eye contact, eyes wandering around my office until they rest at the window settling on the small brown bird perched and noisy on the other side of the glass. I watch that bird bounce around for a second but mostly stay with Ollie's energy, the leather couch crinkling with their subtle movements, their deep sighs.

"My family didn't talk about a lot of things. What little I learned about consent was at school–I remember, maybe in middle school--some teacher saying 'no means no' and that was the extent of it more or less, but it was still more than anyone had EVER told me before and while she was telling us in class, I had a flashback from when I was molested by a peer. No one had ever told me I was allowed to say no...we just didn't talk about those kinds of things in my family. Sitting in class being told about consent was the moment I realized I had trauma and because my first sexual experience was with another kid and everyone still treated me like a boy, I couldn't tell anyone about that flashback. I was already a target. My dad and brothers would've just ran me for it. They treated me like I was gay before I even knew what being gay meant. No one taught me shit about consent but they sure as hell taught me shit about myself."

I feel my own throat constricting, sadness filling my chest cavity as I sit with them. "That sounds achingly hard Ollie...how did you navigate that realization?"

"I tried to fit in. I was such a good kid too, did what I was told. I would've had to be the strong, machismo type you know—been the man, acted rude towards my wife, had to have a fucked up marriage just like my parents, would've had to hide my true self. Even when I tried hard, pretended, it still wasn't enough. Everyone saw me as different and my family made it a point to make me ashamed of it. They couldn't let me be me. So at seventeen I had to leave. I only have my mom now and I worry if I was really myself—if I transitioned fully, I think I might lose her too. I've got myself, but I'm alone. Being myself and having boundaries with my family for the ways they beat on me means I lost them even if what I'm losing isn't good. I'm always choosing between being myself and being hurt by others or being myself and being alone."

"I'm deeply grieved that those have felt like your only options, say more, if you're willing."

"When I think of saying no, I immediately think of loss. I can't afford to be more alone than I already am but also don't want to lose anymore of who I am either. I feel at war with myself all the time because it feels like I'm always losing."

Mel Gentry Bosna

From a young age Ollie both felt different and was treated differently from their siblings and cousins, criticized for being effeminate, harassed more often than not. The experience of being bullied at home continued into school, eventually escalating into acts of violence towards them that their family dismissed and laughed off. They were *"asking for that kind of attention obviously"* were words expressed often.

The internal tension of trying to figure out how to look and act in order for their family to accept them and to feel safe at school constantly activated their nervous system, making it hard to be present and learn in the classroom. This struggle only resulted in another area of vulnerability as they experienced regular criticism from teachers, students and family alike for how they performed at school. They left home at seventeen, moved across state lines, perpetually conflicted with what it costs to be themself versus what it cost them to hide themself.

Their family directly blamed them for any violence they experienced and the rejection that followed was expressed as a 'consequence' for all the multitude of ways they chose to be different which only further isolated them from their community. Pretending to be someone they were not however didn't seem to be enough to keep them safe despite years of trying to blend in. Consider being told you were too feminine and then when you tried to act masculine you were shamed for being fraudulent.

The only fleeting experiences that felt as if they were wanted came from cis gender, otherwise straight-identifying men who fetishized their body and hooked up with them secretly. Setting boundaries around their body, their appearance and the few family members that still talked with them didn't feel like an option as they didn't feel like they could afford to lose anyone else, they already felt alone. When I asked them to define consent they replied "I still don't know what it means for me."

Later in the conversation I affirmed how much safety and belonging I believe them worthy of receiving, how I hope for a world where they don't have to make themself small or be blamed for the harm caused to them simply for existing, and how true I believe their good heart and body to be. I later paused the interview recording so we had space to cry together, I felt honored Ollie shared what they did with me and grieved nonetheless that their trauma had happened.

A House Abandoned

What Ollie experiences is an excruciating dilemma for any one of us to navigate, let alone to ask a child to face and have to resolve. The options of either having to abandon yourself so people accept you or abandon your family in order to safely be yourself are not choices exercised from a place of internal safety and peace, rather it's lacking embodied consent since the underbelly of the decision-making is rooted in deep hurt, scarcity of acceptance and a fear of continued loss—no option feels like a 'win' so what's chosen is the one interpreted to hurt the least.

If we're presented with limited options that force us into a corner, is it any different than being rushed to make a decision with a threat poised at our heart or a noose tied around our neck? We all aim to make the best choice we can discern in any given situation yet must acknowledge we want and deserve better.

In her book Body Work, Melissa Febos writes, "*I want to be awake to all my choices*". I can't help but wonder how different Ollie's life—how different perhaps all of our lives would be if we felt settled and open enough to explore ourselves, safe enough with others to express our discovery of self without threat—to live awake and fully alive without anticipating harm or loss. Perhaps we'd experience our navigation of the world with less of fear's grip, feeling more like who we always hoped ourselves to be. Maybe the world itself would look and feel differently.

Chapter Three

A HUMAN KIND OF MOTHER

I envy the Jesus who died believing humanity could find another world brighter than this one. I prefer his humanity over the divinity of the Christ that holy books have immortalized him into being. If I could, I'd ask Jesus the human and Christ the god-hope to return to Earth as a human mother. To please try in isolation, over and over again to die without promise or certainty of resurrection—to do what I do every damn day, which is to die to myself so my children might live and so I might survive parenting them, all in hope of discovering a world beyond this one other than heaven.

I remember seeing a pie graph that split the experience of parenting nearly in half–51% greatest joy of your life and 49% biggest pain in the ass you're going to experience. I laughed about it then and still think about it now, mostly because those numbers are more fluid than fixed for us and yet nonetheless resonate for me. Admittedly, I find parenting hard. So much so, I often question if it's harder for me than other parents, or, if perhaps I'm just more vocal than other parents about the hard time I'm having. Juries out, however I will say anyone who knows me is privy to the ways in which I wrestle regularly with parenting. Parents aren't supposed to admit this of course, but *especially* mothers are taught to keep their mouths shut about any edges they encounter while mothering. This too has been hard for me, I always seem to have a mouthful.

When mothers struggle, they are often met with internalized misogyny and verbal abuse for not feeling a sense of purpose and joy at the sacrifices involved with raising children. The expectation commonly reinforced for mothers is one of humble gratitude for the opportunity to prioritize the needs of everyone over their own well-being. I'm not sure anyone would say I've done that well, myself included.

Let me be clear: my kids are precious and parenting is exhausting. The reasons I'm stretched belong to me and the systems that perpetuate self-abandonment, they do not belong to my children. In addition to the labor involved with renegotiating expectations set for parents by society, culture and systems of power, I am easily overstimulated by the daily tasks raising small humans requires. There's little room to preserve my own passions and autonomy when everyone has ongoing needs that I've been elected to be in charge of. I'm spent, which is neither my children's fault nor responsibility. It's rooted in complex, multi-faceted systems and relational dynamics.

A few years back I was in a particularly tender season both with parenting and my marriage. I went for a walk after putting everyone to bed. The desert was hot, I was sticky and teary. I noticed how I felt burned out *from the inside*, deeply discouraged, and my least favorite feeling of all–emotionally stuck. I paced my neighborhood which is a common way I try to complete my stress cycle, a practice I learned from Dr. Emily Nagoski and Amelia Nagoski, brilliant researchers and siblings, who co-authored the book *Burnout*.

As I was walking along I heard a car's tires squeal to my left and had this weird wave course through my body, considering the possibilities of what could happen next—I told my good friend Sarah about the walk the following week and she sharply inhaled and asked, "*Did you think of jumping in front of the car?*" She knew how exhausted and burned out I'd been feeling. I startled back– there have been previous seasons in my life in which I'd considered un-aliving myself however that's not what this experience had been.

A House Abandoned

When the car sped up I had this thread of a thought surface, I imagined being the victim of a drive by shooting. That wasn't grounded in any evidence and in itself didn't feel like much data. However, what followed the thought as I remained standing there on the sidewalk unscathed as the car's tail lights drove away was my surprise towards the way I processed the possibility–when I'd considered being shot or hit, I'd felt a wave of relief. I hadn't realized my fatigue was significant enough that, while I didn't want to consciously die, I was utterly heart-spent enough that the idea of no longer having to navigate the daily grind was so goddamn appealing.

I spent the remainder of my walk and the following weeks pulling on these threads, it felt important to understand what lay underneath the exhaustion and annoyance. I started to see how trapped I felt as a parent, especially as a person identifying as and being seen as a mother. I felt powerless in my fatigue, where was there to go, what could I *actually* change as someone already holding so much privilege and resources who still felt this way? What kind of mother fantasizes about leaving, would choose to run away because she wanted more for herself?

I'm well aware of what we say about men who don't stick around, let alone the women who disrupt family systems. I remember as a teenager hearing adults refer to others as losers, deadbeats, home wreckers and the like when they didn't stay in the role society assigned them. The worst message imprinted on me was the description of how *selfish* a parent was for leaving.

To this day I don't hear much curiosity practiced around the dynamics of infidelity, divorce and parents who don't stick around–we're quick to label people as selfish without exploring what's underneath someone wanting, needing or choosing to leave. Are people leaving because they're running *away* from or running *towards* something? I don't support abandonment in any expression and think we're better off practicing compassion and curiosity. What if in doing so we could feel more empowered and have more options allowing us to stick around.

That's exactly what I ended up needing in order to feel less stuck. Not the actual experience of leaving, but permission to do it. Just like I'd previously done with reevaluating my marriage I went ahead and put every kind of parenting option on the table for myself, including disappearing. I trusted my integrity and values enough to not feel threatened by this process—I'd argue that it's only a threat to

39

someone when self-trust is missing. We discourage others from exploring what their feelings and needs are because we fear they're going to choose something we don't approve of–the lack of internal trust manifests as an erosion of relational trust. Turns out that like with my marriage, having the option to leave meant I had an authentic option to stay. If divorce is an option, so is marriage. If abandonment is an option, so is reclamation. If leaving myself is an option, so is coming home to myself.

I'm not the only one who wrestles with this tension. During the COVID-19 pandemic's most collective stage of acute stress, I went for another walk and checked-in on a friend who shared with me how often she'd been fantasizing about being in a car wreck–she also didn't want to die. Her fantasy included an injury just bad enough to warrant a 3-5 day hospital stay so she could get a break from being with her family's needs. She laughed telling me about it, dismissing it as ridiculous and privileged, however I could hear the underlying ache.

That same year I sat in my office with another client I adore. She rotates where she sits when she comes in and I enjoy the mystery week-to-week since it means I get to rotate around the room too. On this particular day she chose the very edge of the couch, perched as though she might want to bolt after her admission, her body seemingly trying to take up as little space as possible on the furniture.

Her brown eyes leveled with mine and right on her exhale I heard her say "*I love my child so, so much. Being a mom is all I ever wanted...turns out though, I really hate motherhood.*"

Tears sprang to my eyes, her eyes, every other mothers' eyes whenever I retell this moment. I was honored she let me witness those opposing yet truthful realities. I still inhale sharply when I reflect on it, understanding that while parenthood has many beautiful seasons, it costs many of us too.

When my own children were younger they were curious about death and the possibility of an afterlife. When we introduced them to the practice of being with life's uncertainties and differing ways people approach living with the unknown, one of my kids asked "*Would you die for us?*" There was safety seeking in that question, they wanted to know if my love was big enough to risk their survival. What they still don't realize is how often I already seemingly do on their behalf.

A House Abandoned

Years spent delaying needs, denying dreams, buttoning up feelings, biting my tongue, all the times I put away untouched food, drive to appointments in rush hour, write the school advocating for support, mediate sibling conflict *everywhere*, revoke privileges that impact my rest more than their pleasure, forsake girls trips for family vacations, replace lazy mornings for screechy cartoons, late dinners for bedtime stories, wake up in the middle of the night because someone can't fall asleep, someone is sick, someone had a bad dream, someone is scared—because I'm scared.

Self-abandonment was how I was taught to be human—it was seen as noble, necessary, always the loving thing to do. Motherhood was packaged in the sacrifice of self, I never saw mothers living wild and free. Instead of 'will you die for us' perhaps a more interesting question to model for kids is this: will I live for you?

Will I find what makes me feel *alive* and pursue it relentlessly? Will I say no to requests from family, the school, from work, from culture? Will I ignore errands, laundry, groceries, volunteering, playdates and emails if it's compromising me—will I say no to mindless drinking, eating, scrolling on my phone? What, whom and when will I choose? Am I willing to leave so I can *consciously stay*— not because it's the 'right' thing or what I signed up for (it's not) but because saving myself is the only death I have power to resurrect.

Perhaps vibrancy best answers our kids' questions. Acknowledging the struggle many of us feel needn't be a character indictment nor minimize the fierce love we have for our families. We're all asked regularly to do the impossible, which is to say, die and resurrect as though it's a rhythm to seasonably follow. What would our family systems look like if we could choose differently?

Giving myself permission to leave completely changed the energy surrounding the ache and powerlessness I'd been bumping up against and while I'm often still fatigued by parenting and the daily routine that comes with it, I'm now a more emotionally grounded parent. I can access and actually feel more options to choose from. I'm less resentful, overall more regulated and decidedly more in alignment with my integrity. I have something to offer my kids because I don't feel chronically stuck and as if they're taking something from me that I'm reluctantly giving. I cannot emphasize it enough—*the whole experience is different*—I'm different.

41

After a decade of parenting, I decided to choose it from a deeper source than obligation ever offered me. When I've shared all of this with my own mother she doesn't seem to relate although she's learning to validate. She seemed to wrestle less in part because she didn't perceive or allow herself to want anything different, anything more—her practice with self-sacrifice came from the cultural and religious expectations to live a small life and she was able to reconcile it. I however, have wanted a life as big as my appetite. Being asked to be content with a smaller life than you crave can feel like another form of gaslighting depending on how and who is doing the asking. Winnowing down societal expectations while expanding my understanding of the need for options led me to redefine self-permission and consent, it empowered me to own my needs and desire for more *while* honoring my kids and marriage.

When it comes to defining a word's definition it's important to ask *who* is defining the concept, what the purpose of editing or expanding a definition intends and why broadening our collective understanding would matter. In other words, not only where did the definition originate from but who is the definition applicable for and *most importantly*, who gains power and therefore protection from its evolution.

I state this again as I don't presume to have your trust and also because the challenge to examine the power of a word's meaning and its practice ought to merit our curiosity. I'll share my thoughts throughout the book regarding how I define these definitions and practices, however in order to better delineate what I believe an embodied, integrated consent practice to be it's important for reference to start with what it isn't. Many of us grow up lacking a definition and understanding around consent, the absence of this erodes our safety and perpetuates ongoing boundary violations throughout our lives as we're disconnected from our intuition and bodies.

From those I interviewed, the few participants who *had* been offered a definition of consent primarily learned it through sex education at their public school. It was almost exclusively applied to sex and almost always outlined in a binary framework of 'yes means yes/no means no.'

There are places that having a rigid delineation of consent's boundaries absolutely matters, for instance in a court of law. Sexual violence, harassment and misconduct are hard enough to prove with the ways the United States' justice system operates, there is no allowance for expanding our definitions to include nuance and complexity despite the reality that we deserve it. The United States' justice system utilizes a punitive rather than reparative framework. Until our institutions and communities reevaluate how we relate to and value each other, we can anticipate binary frameworks being what we're offered and solutions for accountability and repair remaining inadequate with returning us to safety and belonging.

In more recent years there's been a cultural shift with language around consent, again due to the #MeToo movement and the intentional efforts of activists and educators who are creating a more comprehensive consent culture—sex positivity and inclusivity are the pillars within this evolving framework. Increasingly, a more common description of consent within this movement is the term enthusiastic consent, meaning if it's not a 'HELL YES, it's a no.' I was initially enthralled with this concept as it felt counterculture from the mediocre definitions previously given and I loved the idea of enthusiasm being used as the benchmark.

That changed however as I regarded the myriad of ways I show up in my own life and make choices from a place of integrity but admittedly lacking in enthusiasm. For instance, how many of us have woken up in the middle of the night to have to care for a sick child, came home to a mess made by a pet, received a last minute but legitimate ask from our supervisor, perhaps even had half-assed, tired sex with a partner we love and decided to lean in and be present for—we often can align with our values, despite the vacancy of enthusiastic energy, or at least I have.

If enthusiasm is what defines consent, how then do we categorize all the other choices we make that we discern to be 'right' because of our values but that are also clearly lacking excitement? How do we make sense of the reality that parts of us can feel enthusiastic and willing while other parts feel restricted, even cautious around the same opportunity or 'ask' of us. How can we explain and reconcile the conflicts that exist within us, let alone simply to words such as, '*yes means yes, no means no*'?

I define consent as relating to the amount of mindful presence we have with ourselves and the degree to which we have both awareness of what we're feeling and access to being able to express our needs, desires and boundaries. It's about discerning what parts are saying '*yes, no and maybe*', being able to be present with our bodies so we can discern which parts of us want to lean in and which want to hide away. It's giving ourselves permission to be able to express our inner world even if and when it disrupts others, it's staying with our values and needs, refusing to abandon our inner knowing because we understand the costs of not doing so is far too great. In essence–it's about being home, embodied with ourselves.

In *Girlhood*, Melissa Febos writes about her experience with empty consent and the ways she experimented differently at a cuddle party she attended in New York. Like many of us, she had experienced situations throughout her life that felt harmful but that she didn't feel were quantifiably traumatic.

> *I do not have a definitive proposal for what should constitute abuse and what should not. More expert people have made this their work. What I do have is growing certainty about the ways in which I have collaborated in the mistreatment of my own body. What I have is the will and freedom and resources to stop harming myself in the subtle ways I have been conditioned. If I have learned anything from my study of empty consent, it is that I must turn on the lights and welcome every part of me into the room. If I want my yes to mean yes, there can be no locked doors in the house of me.*

I read *Girlhood* in the summer of 2021 sandwiched between my kids on a full airplane on our way to Lake Michigan, tears streaming down my cheeks. I had spent the previous few years working out my own practice of an internal, awakened consent and yet had never had another writer mirror with such clarity what empty consent feels like nor penned language that offered an alternative practice.

As I continued experimenting with my own embodied consent practice, I found myself repeating those five, fresh, vibrating words into a meditation: *In The House Of Me.*

A House Abandoned

Later that fall an artist tattooed the word 'home' beautifully over my heart as a reminder for those moments when I temporarily depart from myself. It's an altar etched on my body, inviting me to return, rest, replenish and then explore. I can trust what I feel and discover within and I believe you can too.

Chapter Four

RECLAIMING A BODY

"Embodiment is our birthright, it's our coming home, a remembering of our wholeness."

–Dr. Hilary McBride, PhD

A vibrant consent practice starts with internal alignment–it's the ability to be with ourselves without terror of what we'll discover inside, the readiness to explore our own inner territory. It seeks to listen patiently, honors needs, feelings, and when parts inside of us are in conflict, the practice discerns what our highest self would choose as our safest and wisest option and defers to it. In essence, a fuller consent practice is about self-alignment.

The alternative experience many of us share is one of disembodiment, best explained as feeling disconnected from our bodies. Disembodiment is heightened space from parts of self that are present but separate from each other. The separation of our inner world while we're *simultaneously* participating in the outer world is what contributes to the practice of empty consent. It's what happens when we're not awake enough to our bodies and intuition and therefore give permission from a place of default participation. We say *'yes'* because it's what's expected, *'yes'* because it's a habit, *'yes'* because we're not connected to the parts of us that perhaps feel differently.

Empty consent can also happen when we *are* aware of our inner world however due to feeling too much is at stake with sharing it, we default to an expected response such as what Ollie did as a child—they knew who they were and how they wanted to express themselves yet didn't feel safe enough to do so. Sometimes empty consent comes from unawareness of ourselves and sometimes it comes with awareness but in a void of safe relationships to practice a healthier consent—both types of default consent cause harm.

From my experience as a clinician, disembodiment happens when we disconnect from our bodies with the intention of avoiding conflict, emotions, sensation or somatically stored memory. This can be conscious avoidance or an unconscious, internalized pattern we're not aware we're participating in. We may be mentally engaged and seemingly present in the outer world, however we aren't in touch with our bodies and therefore miss the information our bodies are offering us about what we're experiencing.

When I work with a client, I often invite them to notice what's happening in their body as they're processing a specific belief or emotion and may ask if they can locate where the sensation or a memory appears to be stored. For someone prone to disembodiment it's common to feel disconnected, even bewildered by the symptoms their body is experiencing, especially if the avoidance or compartmentalization of self isn't a practice they are engaging in consciously.

I've noticed dissociation often used interchangeably with disembodiment and I'd like to briefly delineate the differences as I understand them. Disembodiment is a lack of connection or presence with our bodies, dissociation is a wider separation of self due to a higher level of emotional overwhelm or threat we're experiencing. Our bodies and more specifically our brains and nervous systems make a split second interpretation when we experience something as unsafe or perceived as a threat. This may not always be helpful however it is what our bodies do nonetheless on our behalf.

Dissociation is a purposeful response and part of our physiology and bodily wisdom. Despite the fact that dissociation often gets a bad rap in mental health spaces, in and of itself it's not a bad thing. There are times and experiences where dissociating from what's happening is, in fact, *our safest option*. Many people describe the experience as disappearing or floating–they may feel blank, experience time and space fuzzing for a bit or observe what's happening from a bird's eye view, almost as though whatever is happening is impacting someone else and not themselves.

Dissociation may be an appropriate, adaptive response to trauma when we can't get away from whatever unsafe thing is happening and exposing us to harm. It's the way our bodies dial down and preserve both our energy and the integrity of our core self until we later have a chance to return to ourselves and escape. Dissociation can become problematic however when it develops into a default stress response and we find ourselves dissociating in situations where *we need* to be present in order to access our intuition, power, consent and boundaries. When we default to dissociation whenever we feel something emotionally charged or uncomfortable surface we may end up compromising our safety even though the intention of our bodies all along is to help us survive and eventually return us to safety.

Disconnecting from our bodies happens in sync with the denial of our stories. Most of my clients begin exploring embodiment as a practice during our time together and initially express difficulty locating or being with the emotions and sensations that come up as they're learning how to be more present with themselves. While it's an unfamiliar practice for most of us who are learning, it's an altogether disruptive experience for my clients who have more complex trauma and regularly experience dissociation as a way of navigating the symptoms of their C-PTSD. I aim to structure an intentional rhythm in our work which incrementally honors each person's limits and capacity, and even then it often happens where emotions or memories a client isn't yet ready to feel or explore becomes activated prematurely. When that's the case it's important to use skills to help reorient to the time and place we're in.

These skills include grounding through using our senses to come back to the present and our bodies (for instance, the 5-4-3-2-1 Grounding Technique). If it's actually not safe enough to be in the present because something bad is happening, our brains default to protective threat responses such as dissociation, intellectualization or compartmentalization in order to help us dial down the intensity and ultimately, to help us survive however we can.

Mel Gentry Bosna

I ask my clients to identify their favorite wall art in the office (sight), notice the bird chirping at the windowsill (sound), the way the couch or rug feel beneath them (touch), and what their beverage flavor is (taste and smell). Through conversation we'll start talking about something unrelated to the previous intense emotion as a way of coming back to the present and back to their body in a way that feels more manageable. This incremental return to safety is important and one I encourage all of us to use when our stress or emotions feel bigger than we can comfortably manage.

I found myself practicing this with Jade who had previously denied any history of trauma despite exhibiting symptoms consistent with C-PTSD. She and I had been working with each other for over a year. Initially she came to my office to try and work on her preoccupation with her body and the restrictive nutritional habits she engaged in to manage her distress around it.

Jade is a lot of fun to talk with, she is wickedly sarcastic, thoughtful, feels deep empathy for animals and has a resiliency that she spends a large amount of time minimizing from my perspective. I've listened to women for decades talk about their bodies as though they are somehow both the problem and solution to their pain. I have zero judgment about this however admittedly get bored with the conversation if we don't eventually explore the underbelly of their ache—my clients and friends know this about me as I don't take long before I start to pull on the threads I hear in conversation about their bodies and dieting practices.

One cloudy afternoon, Jade plopped her purse down, sank into the corner of the couch and began a familiar dialogue with me about how disgusting her body is. I watched her fingers play with the tassels on my turquoise pillow as she began a familiar lament about her thighs, her stomach, her neck. For or a moment I was preoccupied with the movement of her hands on the threads of the pillow as I wondered how many people have played with the tassels, braided them, used them to soothe the discomfort of talking about vulnerable things. Jade and I have talked often enough about her body dissatisfaction for me to know that it's the symptom of deeper underlying wounds.

Eventually we bump up against it in this conversation when she shares how she's been experimenting with ways of dissociating less–we'd previously been working on how to recognize when it may compromise her safety to dissociate versus when it might actually be a safer option.

A House Abandoned

"One of the things I'd love for you to play around with is giving yourself more options than dissociating or white knuckling the experiences you're having" I offered.

She drew a long breath, "*What do you mean by options?*" Her eyes momentarily meet mine before skipping over to the bookshelf she's perused a hundred times already.

"It seems often enough the only options that present themselves in uncomfortable or scary moments are either to float away through dissociation or, to white knuckle and force yourself to endure whatever hard thing is happening. I'd love for you to have more than two options in addition to also having *kinder* options than those two—otherwise there's an increased risk of you not being able to practice consent." As I reflect this I notice she is visibly becoming more agitated, her fingers more anxiously pulling the tassel threads.

I continue, softening my tone further, watching her body's language as it's offering me more data than her words are currently. "If we only have two options to choose between and neither one of them actually *feels* very safe or what we'd want to choose, there's a good chance we're not able to access or express consent from safe alignment. Sometimes when something bad is happening it's absolutely necessary to dissociate and freeze but overall white-knuckling things wouldn't be how we'd safely navigate through life."

I pause, letting the space fill before gently adding, "I want more for you".

At this point Jade's hands weren't the only part of her communicating that her body was activated—she was shifting on the couch and started breathing more anxiously, her words first frozen and then quickly flooding out, "*I have NEVER had sex with ANYONE while present in my body. Like, not once...are you saying that I haven't consented to sex with my partner?!*"

I then understood what realization was surfacing for her and that she appeared to be approaching a state of emotional flooding which Jade often experiences right before she dissociates or has a panic attack. She deserved support and needed help grounding rather than exploring any further what we'd started talking about which is precisely then what we pivoted to. Through breathing, the 5-4-3-2-1 grounding technique and generalized distraction we shifted the conversation outward and Jade's nervous system began to settle, I could see her body and mood relax and reset.

Later in the session I practiced containing the tender realization that had surfaced earlier, saying "We bumped a layer today that felt too big and really unfamiliar—I'm grateful for the way your body communicated that limit to both of us so we were able to set it aside for perhaps another season you feel more ready to safely explore it. We both know it's there, we're not pretending, it can stay wherever you want to container it indefinitely. Hopefully we eventually go back and heal that layer, however we're never going to intentionally go back for it before you feel ready."

We take a deep breath together, and her wandering eyes meet mine as we exhale, I mean the following words when I say them, "I promise to wait".

We tabled it and started incrementally working on ways she could practice giving herself more than two restrictive options in other areas of her life. Months went by and Jade started coming in excited to share how giving herself more options with work, social activities, family boundaries and travel was increasing her sense of power and providing more safety than she'd previously felt.

A year later we were able to pull that internal container back out with an approach that felt significantly less threatening as she now had evidence that she could practice curiosity around having or creating more options and in turn offer herself permission and safety by adding in additional choices still. The way we talked around the container and what it held became a flow we practiced together and in so doing, were able to honor each session's limits and Jade's capacity in a way that reduced harm.

I know from personal experience how it feels to have someone violate a limit. Years back I was between therapists when a particularly disruptive crisis happened in my life. The therapist I had been working with had recently left on maternity leave and I was desperate and reached out to a therapist I'd worked with years prior. I was hoping she could squeeze me in, even if only for temporary support. I met with her the following week and when I think back to the session, I can recognize how she intended to help—I don't doubt it in fact. However her advice seemed hell-bent on me 'getting' the severity of the situation I was in more than anything else, almost as though she was worried I was going to stay disembodied or live in denial.

A House Abandoned

In the process of making sure her points landed, I felt harmed, going as far as to say that my conversation with her felt *more traumatic* for my body than the actual crisis I was navigating outside of therapy.

I ended my time with her feeling more panicked than when I'd started the session. All I could do was text my friends as my body seemed like it was navigating between an anxiety attack and guttural sobs. Christine was the first friend to respond and I sat shaking in my car, sobbing while she listened, eventually she offered a third-way. *"I'm here. What the counselor said is one way to look at your life, there are other ways too. We'll find another one."*

Christine reminded me there were options even if we didn't know yet what they were. I had time to find my path and be with my pain, time to explore which options I was willing to try. She pointed me back to myself instead of rushing me towards a path she thought I needed to take. She honored where I was–albeit snotty and hyperventilating and was willing to be *with* me instead of strong-arming me somewhere she thought I should go. I felt cared for instead of managed, I hung up that call with no real solutions yet however felt significantly less alone.

I never followed up with that therapist again nor do I refer to her or anyone else who I hear practices a rushed therapeutic process. When reflecting on earlier stages of my career, I can see where I participated in harm this way too, either by missing a client's limits or by assessing that therapeutically it was important to continue processing something a client wasn't ready or willing to hear. I was trained clinically to engage in a process of rupture and repair in this particular way and yet now deeply regret it. I am committed to owning it, repairing it and showing up differently now that I can discern and align better.

Even in a crisis, I believe we are better off having people willing to pause with us where we're at in the process–in fact, many times the reason people often rush through a crisis, whether ours or their own, is due to the emotional distress experienced feeling *so damn intolerable.* We cannot be present with someone else's pain if we haven't learned how to be present with our own fears, wounds and healing. Emotion, ours *or* others, can present like a threat to our bodies that we reactively avoid or destroy unless we're able to see it as a part of the whole landscape. We are not only capable of handling life's challenges and our big feelings, but healing our wounds as well.

Mel Gentry Bosna

Perhaps it's what's too often missing—we need more people willing to stand in our corner with steady hands at our back then we will ever need in front of us with scorching torches showing us the way. Perhaps if we trust each other, we could embody a gentle safety and become bridges of honesty and connection so those around us discover options that eventually lead to sanctuary. That's certainly what Christine offered me. She didn't have advice or solutions, she was present, reminding me I would be okay, even and especially in the moment I couldn't yet feel that I was going to be okay. It was a precious gift and supported me with eventually finding a way forward with learning how to access internal consent.

If you've experienced harm in a place that's supposed to be safe, be it in a therapist or doctor's office, hospital, family gathering, school classroom or inside a church youth group, if you've ever felt pressure to share your body, your story or your feelings before you were ready, if no alternative options were afforded you in the middle of your pain, I need you to hear this—you are not alone. Many of us have experienced coercion offered as help, it's valid to acknowledge and grieve it's impact.

I'm painfully aware of the particular ache of being pried open. You're allowed to run from anyone who acts entitled to your vulnerability. You don't need permission to protect your story in the same way you don't need anyone's permission to save your life. If we want to feel present in our bodies and heal our stories, we need to trust that when we're invited to share ourselves that what we disclose will be cared for with the respectfulness our sacred sharing deserves through a process we get to govern for ourselves.

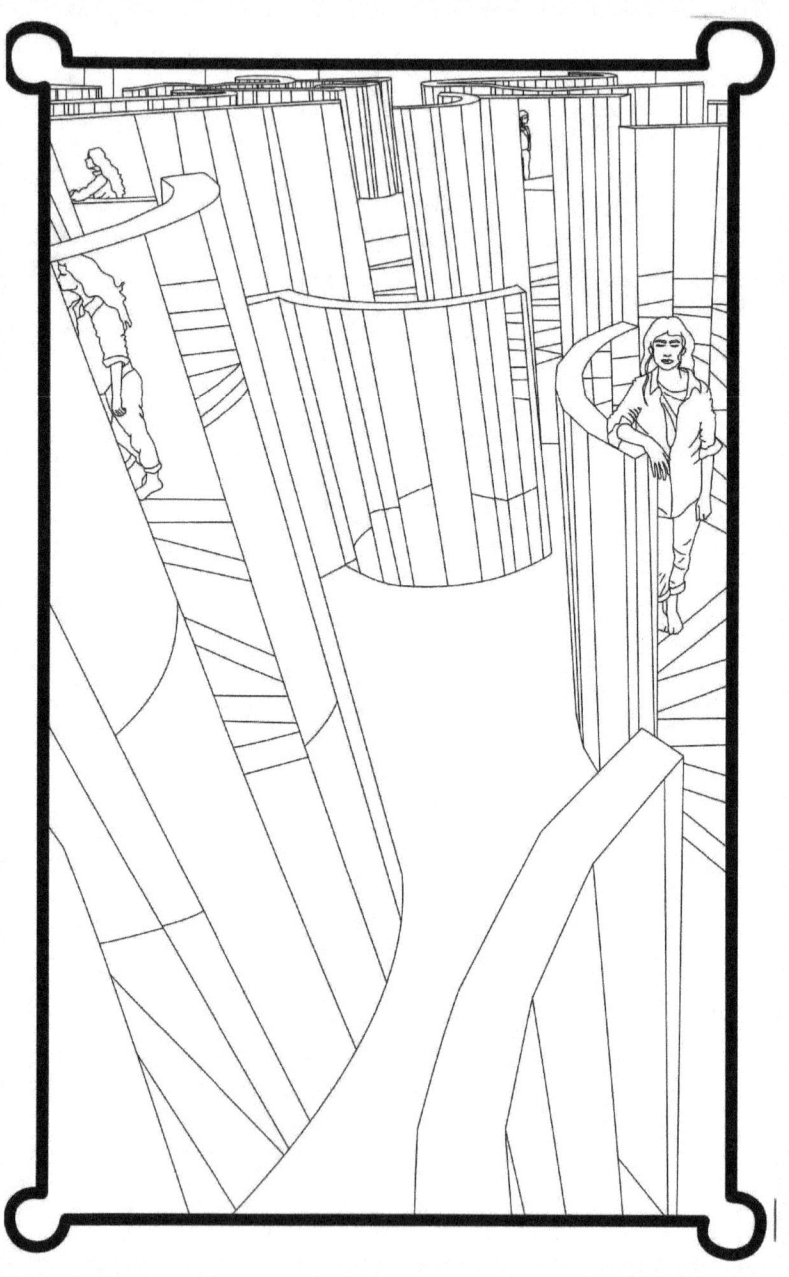

Part II: A House Of Mirrors

"I think each family has a funhouse logic all its own, and in that distortion, in that delusion, all behavior can seem both perfectly normal and crazy."

—Darin Strauss

"Madness plants mirrors in the desert. I find the means frightening."

—Floriano Martins

Chapter Five

SYSTEMS THAT HIJACK CONSENT

"I feel so goddamn robbed" Jade says minutes into the session. There's a layer of irritation that feels new, her words hold a heat to them and I notice the ways they energize the space.

I listen, curious about what's underneath the anger and notice a split that seems to be happening within her. She's sitting cross-legged on the jute rug on my office floor while playing with the therapy puppy, Mr. Rainbow, a miniature labradoodle whom we all seem to be a *tad-too-obsessed* with. Jade is one of his favorite visitors, as she's running her fingers playfully through Bowie's fur I notice the sharp contrast of the tension on her face, irritation in her voice and the playfulness of her hands on his body.

She repeats herself, this time her voice breaking harder as tears follow the guttural statement: *"I FEEL ROBBED."*

"Say more if you can," I lean forward in my chair, anticipating more words and feelings coming.

Mel Gentry Bosna

Jade has done remarkable work this year with increasing both her capacity and ability to be with herself in longer and more frequent doses, which means when I now ask this question she can access more of herself and name parts of her story that previously felt unsafe to explore let alone heal. She's steadily been roaming the perimeter of her inner world and history, a practice that in other seasons was too overwhelming and would lead to dissociation.

"For the first time in my life I feel like I can consent to sex–now I'm with a partner I want to be with who is good to me, which I'm grateful—but I can't stop thinking of all those goddamn years I disappeared and left my body. All that time feels utterly wasted. I'm so mad my family didn't get me help when I needed it, the signs of my trauma were always there–they KNEW and no one helped, and growing up in purity culture made it SO much worse!

Any chance I could've had with a normal sex life was completely wrecked by my church so instead of anyone helping me feel safe, everyone in my life–my parents, youth leaders and the dumb-fuckers at that Christian school just made me feel even MORE ashamed which I didn't even think was possible. I'm so fucking MAD. I'm 33 years old and what–am I going to leave the best relationship I've ever been in just because my teenage self didn't get to sleep around?! Damnit Mel. I'm mad and so, so sad for myself. I feel utterly robbed of normal. I can't get it back."

Jade's crying heavily at this point, the puppy is still in her lap and I'm softly and silently crying too. I take this moment to be with her grief, a practice she's learned this year we can do together where previously we would've exclusively utilized grounding skills in order to set the intensity of her emotions aside.

She's referencing a part of her trauma we'd only recently started exploring, specifically how her religious upbringing has informed rigid practices around her body, sexuality and within her relationships without, of course, her consent. I hear this commonly from my clients and it was repeatedly expressed by the participants I interviewed–hell, I hear this commonly within my own community of friends and colleagues–those of us who were raised with shame and fear as the primary guides of our development.

At best it's a lingering frustration with reconciling the choices many of us seemingly made before we knew that alternative paths existed. Recognizing the absence of consent in our lives can trigger grief as we process losses we may not previously have been able to identify. Andrea Gibson, brilliant poet and spoken word artist writes, *"Praise the moment when our grief becomes a window, when we can see what we could not see before."* I love this line, offering it to myself when a moment of clarity about the past presents itself–we can eventually behold these moments with praise after we experience them as portals into self-reclamation. First though, we face what caused the loss and this reckoning can be wildly disruptive and heartbreaking.

Engaging in grief while honoring our capacity to be *with* loss is a necessary experience and one that can synchronize with the rebuilding we do in areas we previously experienced empty consent. If we want to actually choose who we are and resurrect a life worth living, we must eventually revisit the places in our history where 'no trespassing signs' were placed by ourselves or others, a concept introduced to me first by writer Jaiya John. With compassion we practice curiosity surrounding parts of ourselves that were barricaded away, perhaps left as condemned or burned on an altar. We notice the other paths people followed that were marked as dangerous and off-limits for us, understanding now why our bodies and hearts never regarded them as options.

Developing a vibrant, embodied consent invites us to face the grief that walking paths void of consent has cost us. While we can reclaim our beliefs and bodies and eventually rewrite the scripts we live by, none of those foundational experiences are returned to us unmarked. The grief Jade and others have brought into my office as they've waded through the impact of empty consent and outright harm is no small thing–grief and trauma are beasts to recover from.

I hope when you lean into reclaiming parts of yourself impacted by trauma and loss, that you experience it in the company of safe people. If you do not feel like you currently have someone safe enough, I hope you continue searching as no one deserves to feel alone—you, dear reader, do not deserve to be alone.

In order to develop an embodied consent practice, grieve the parts of ourselves lost and resurrect a life and identity worth living, we must do two things: one, consider the individual experiences that prevented us from accessing options, and two, examine the broader systems that hijack our consent development to begin with. In this section I'd like to address the institutions I recognize intentionally delay consent development and how these specific systems operate from a 'power-over' model therefore benefitting from our collective dissociation and disembodiment: patriarchy, religious fundamentalism and white supremacy.

I'm less invested in providing a detailed, historical account of each institutional power as authors with far more expertise have already produced this work, however I am committed to sharing real, human stories from my research and how I interpret the harmful impact these systems have on consent development and expression. These systems erode autonomy, agency and our communities safety as they intentionally disconnect us from our intuition, self-trust and right to self-govern. They harm all individuals and communities they encounter.

Patriarchy

"patriarchy has no gender." –bell hooks

I'm twelve minutes into an interview and the office is quiet, cool. It's early spring and the morning light is soft and somehow invitational. I softly inhale, curious as to how this participant will respond to the next question. This is my fifteenth interview to date with the study and so far each person's response to this particular question has fallen under a general umbrella of answers.

The participant and I are around the same age, grew up in the same city, both white, raised in evangelical church culture, married, parenting elementary age kids, both working in therapeutic spaces–one could say we have both broad and specific overlaps of life, checking many of the same boxes. Someone else might sing along, *'same, same, same–but different.'* This participant is a cis man.

"What do you remember learning about consent when you were growing up, if you learned anything at all?"

His brow furrows for a second, broad shoulders shrug loosely, he sighs and says casually, "*nothing*".

Noah's energetic and confident so his reply of '*nothing*' wasn't how I expected this extroverted human to answer. I wait and when nothing more follows, I continue. "If the answer to what you learned initially about consent was '*nothing*', how has your definition of consent evolved—how would you define it today?"

He's contemplative, drinks from his water bottle, furrows his brows again and responds: "*It's scary now to me that I wasn't told what consent was. I'm a cisgender male—I've been an athlete much of my life, you'd think someone might've taught me something. Now that I'm thinking more about it, I guess I'd say I've mostly learned that I live in a world that does not require my consent.*"

He continues but I've already stopped taking notes, my own breath momentarily halted in my body. I'm grateful the interview is being recorded since parts of me just became activated. While I want to lean in, stay present, I know myself well enough by now to honor and prioritize what's happening inside *my own body* in addition to paying attention to his body and words.

He leans forward on my couch.

I feel uncertain about defining consent, even now. I've learned more about it through culture, mostly the news, some of it my therapeutic training. Still, defining consent seems awkward—I can see that it's surprising and seems unnecessary to a lot of men, annoying to others that they could be perceived as the bad guy. I think most guys like me think of past relationships, sex and may never recognize the places consent wasn't practiced since we weren't looking for it to begin with.

I look back now on my adolescence and the experience of being in a literal locker room surrounded by other dudes, being absolutely stunned as my teammates described rape without, like, knowing it, rape was just so...common. No one seemed to know they were doing it or at least cisgender, straight dudes didn't seem to know how often they were doing it. For instance, they could tell a girl wasn't all that into something or was piss-ass drunk, but not seem to connect it meant she wasn't consenting. For sure no dude was talking about having THEIR consent violated because that would never have been a thing to admit to. I don't even think guys knew they should be asked for consent too.

At this point I remind myself to exhale, breath work is one of the primary ways to settle a triggered body, inhaling can be more activating, a slow, steady exhale communicates to the body that we are safe enough to return to calm. I don't feel unsafe with Noah—I'm not activated by his presence as much as I felt the honest brutality of his disclosure. I enjoy talking with him, he's here, participating in a study on consent, as best as I can tell he's pursuing collective healing and reckoning with his own power and privileged status. He seems curious about the ways in which his life experience has been shaped by patriarchy's narrow definition of masculinity.

My body's response isn't connected as much to what's happening during this interview as much as it's responding to what many of us know and already understand: Good men uphold patriarchy and participate in misogyny. In fact many of the men we know and are in relationship with whom we'd call good men participate in rape, be it directly, passively or by benefiting from a culture that sustains it.

Men we know, love and often adore, have parts that engage in violence—passively at best and actively enough. Men we otherwise trust and are in close relationship with protect rape culture, not because of their intentions to harm but often due to their passivity surrounding the dynamics of unchallenged power—this allows men to stay unaware of their power until it's challenged, oblivious to the vulnerabilities of others and, dangerously, permits the assumption of equity when it comes to consent as a reciprocal practice.

I'm reminded of a quote from Judith Lewis Herman, "...*In practice the standard for what constitutes rape is set not at the level of women's experience of violation but just above the level of coercion acceptable to men.*"

It bears repeating: while intention matters, intention alone will never be enough to ensure that consent is actually happening due to the ways power works in the world. Impact, meaning the harm that results *regardless* of intention, is what causes trauma. This also merits repeating: not a single one of us chooses *how* we're impacted. We don't get to cognitively select or dismiss the ways in which an experience imprints on our body any more than we choose our trauma responses. Presuming equity when one holds a position of power is a dangerous, reckless practice.

We cannot dismantle rape culture without first building consent culture, we cannot do either of those necessary tasks without tackling the beast of patriarchy and returning to individual and collective embodiment practices. The world needs men to lean harder and more honestly into the underbelly of *why* and *how* they benefit from the system, participate in it and perpetuate harm. Toxic

masculinity and rape culture are guaranteed outcomes of patriarchal structure–
we must dismantle patriarchy further still by asking why and how all genders,
women included, support and enable toxic masculinity as well.

Perhaps the biggest deception by patriarchy is the confusion surrounding whom
it impacts–the reality is, no one wins. No one is left unharmed by a system that
asks the world's entire population to live disembodied, unaware and unchecked.
No one wins when we socialize men to depart from their inner compass and live
in such a way that men, intentionally or not, deny the sovereignty of others'
agency to self-navigate. No one wins, including men.

I return to Noah's story on my exhale, coming back to his last admission, asking
again "how has your definition of consent evolved?"

*"It's embarrassing to me it's taken this long but it's coming together–through
pop culture, media, educational campaigns at universities, like–literal women's
groups holding up signs saying 'don't rape anyone' was a wake-up call because
I realize the way I was raised was to think of rape as only violent assault by a
stranger. I realize now that more teens and twenty year adolescents need to hear
what it actually is and learn more about consent. I assume most cisgender,
heterosexual men do not have ANY conception of consent other than that it
means there's something happening we can't get away with anymore."*

He pauses, reflecting on his own words as they hang between us, *"I think that's
limited but a pretty common understanding men have of consent now."*

As Noah names a reality that most men, or hell, *most people* don't talk about
openly, I take the moment to again notice what's happening inside my body, how
the energy has moved around, felt big at times, settled at others, and decide to
reflect my own attunement to him: "What does talking about this feel like for
you? Do you experience this anywhere in your body when you reflect or share
about it?"

He smiles, open, friendly, seemingly willing to continue our conversation and
says, *"Nah...I don't feel anything in my body."*

I blink, pause as I consider what his last statement means and its general
implication for accessing, giving and receiving consent..."so what you're
saying is that this is more of an intellectual observation?"

Mel Gentry Bosna

He nods and we move onto question number four.

The interview validated what I'd been wrestling with for years–the space between what we know, understand and *actually* practice regarding consent, body autonomy, personal agency and boundaries is what ultimately determines how safe we're able to keep ourselves and others. Our knowledge is only as effective as our actual integration and direct expression of our inner world and our generous assumption and deference that others have an inner world that exists and is worth inquiring about. Consent practices only protect us when we know how to listen and process what's going on *inside* us and also understand how to ask, listen to and honor others as well.

People often overlook the influence systemic power has on our individual and collective development. I'd argue many valid reasons exist that warrant deconstructing the foundational ideologies we've collectively grown up within. Patriarchy may be an obvious system causing us harm, however if we don't take time to consider the specific ways in which it reverberates in our communities, and specifically in our bodies, we will continue to enable it rather than transform it.

In *Understanding Patriarchy*, bell hooks defines toxic masculinity as an extension of patriarchal values, naming the impact patriarchy has on all of our development including its negative impact on men:

> *Patriarchy is the single most life-threatening social disease assaulting the male body and spirit in our nation. Yet most men do not use the word "patriarchy" in everyday life. Most men never think about patriarchy—what it means, how it is created and sustained.... Men who have heard and know the word usually associate it with women's liberation, with feminism, and therefore dismiss it as irrelevant to their own experiences.*

A House Of Mirrors

I include this quote for multiple reasons, one of which is that it mirrors a patterned response I received from cisgender, heterosexual men in my interviews when I asked them to define consent. In general most the interviewees regardless of race, sex and background shared similar experiences of being offered inadequate definitions of consent when they were growing up, however some have since been able to evolve their definition into a deeper understanding and current practice with consent and boundaries. The response of many cis, straight white men however landed in juxtaposition to the group as a whole–not because these men verbalized an alternative definition but because most responded initially with blank stares and silence, initially offering no definition at all.

Danger and vulnerability exists in direct proportion to the ways in which systems protect those already in positions of protected power by enabling unchecked unawareness, fragility and the subsequent wrongdoing caused as a result. The position of not having to consider patriarchy in general nor consent specifically perpetuates default patterns of interacting with others as though intention is equitable to impact and we're all afforded and able to access the same amount of safety.

When asked what initial definition he was given of consent and what his definition is today, another male participant blinked three times before replying, *"I mean...I just have to make sure to get it."*

Yet another male participant described a situation as a young adolescent where he watched a friend of his have *"consensual sex with his girlfriend"*. Later on the girl accused his friend of assault and he wasn't able to defend him out of fear that accusations could be made against him even as well, even though the sex had been consensual from his perspective. I pointed out that while the sex between the two parties may have been consensual (I had no way of determining this one way or another, it was clear there hadn't been consideration of her consent with being watched while having sex, therefore a boundary violation had nonetheless occurred even if an assault had not.

Even if she wildly and enthusiastically had sex with his friend, even if the accusation she made were false, even if the sex was consensual and something she later regretted, etc. a red flag was still present: anyone who viewed her having sex without her explicit permission to do so was violating consent. The *"hmph"* sound the participant made followed by a gentle pause seemed to indicate he was processing, perhaps weighing consent as necessary outside of/in addition to the direct experience of the parties involved in the acts of sex. Even if no one directly intended harm to her, a boundary was trespassed nonetheless. As we talked I could see a part of him recognize the power dynamics of permission while other parts seemed to minimize them all together—this is not uncommon from the experiences I've had with men.

After a violation has occurred, we often allow a person's intentions to make an appearance, using them as a way of exonerating those (men) involved as though good or neutral intentions are enough. Harm remains a predictable outcome of boundary and consent violations regardless of intent and the system of patriarchy does not require men to be awake enough to consider either.

Patriarchy's missteps are not always as obvious or directly aggressive. Sometimes the discrepancy between intent and impact takes on less overt forms, leaving many of us scratching our heads wondering why something bothered us so. A few years back I attended a professional meeting with a group of local mental health professionals. We were exploring how to make therapeutic services more accessible for vulnerable communities in Arizona.

I walked into a small office with a half dozen other professionals and a man turned towards me as I walked in, exuberant and friendly in his greeting. My back was already pressed to the door with nowhere to turn after entering. He was friendly, loud and warm in his greeting and despite the fact we had never been close, despite the fact that it had been eighteen plus years since we'd last interacted, despite it being a professional space, he proceeded to ask me if it was okay to hug me. Everyone else in the small room had paused their conversations and watched our interaction (perhaps I imagined it, *I certainly felt it*).

I remember the split second pause, different parts of my body sending signals, firing off while I processed the options and the subsequent scenarios that might play out. The room and gathering was small enough where everyone present would have watched our interaction and to any outsider, he was doing the right thing by asking me for permission before leaning in for a hug—so why did I pause? What felt wrong about his question?

The reality is that while he did ask for permission which is what we're often encouraging men to do, I couldn't access my own consent fast enough nor did I feel directly comfortable enough to express it in front of others. My body was acutely aware of the door handle's presence on my back, feeling like I had nowhere to go. My mind felt tuned to the measurements of the room, the reality that if I was assertive or perceived as aggressive, I'd be sitting with this small group of professionals nonetheless for the next two plus hours brainstorming options for mental health treatment. Regardless of how society matures, I felt acutely aware of how people broadly misinterpret women's boundaries as an overreach. That knowing coupled with the fact the individual asking was tall, broad-shouldered, white, cisgender, heterosexual and standing within three feet of me with neither one of us having anywhere to go, I found myself defaulting to an old trauma pattern of saying '*yes*' to his request when every part of me wanted to say '*no.*'

It was an expression of default, empty consent, my body resorted to the pathway of least resistance and I caved. Afterward I spent time processing it, deeply curious about myself. It certainly didn't seem like he meant any harm—his wife was in the room as were other mutual friends and colleagues. I gently questioned my self-abandonment, trying to discern why I hadn't felt safe enough to kindly stick out my hand and respond with a simple "I'll pass on the hug but gladly take a handshake."

I was forgetting the wisdom of my body and trauma responses, how, at the end of the day, both are looking out for me and will always default to what appears safest in any given moment—even *if* it wasn't most in alignment. I felt no judgment towards myself, simply frustration for the seemingly obligated public hug I participated in that I hadn't wanted to receive. The more access and self-compassion I experienced, the more I was able to accept how I responded and where I was at, landing in a place of hope that the next time I was in a similar position I might be able to show up differently on my own behalf.

That reflection freed me however the fact he asked me for a hug in the first place continued to bother me. I found myself sifting through questions: Did he offer a hug to every other colleague who walked in? Only to the female therapists? I followed that thread and started wondering if he offered his clients a hug at the end of their sessions–which ones does he offer a hug to? It felt an important consideration as his office was small, the work of therapy, especially trauma therapy, is vulnerable by nature. A power differential automatically exists between therapists and their clients, a power differential between cisgender, straight white men and literally *everyone* else automatically exists. I cycled around those thoughts for a bit because regardless of his intentions the potential impact for a relational disruption felt present at best and harmful at worst.

People might write off that above example as being another reason to eye roll the exaggerations of our current movement. I can already hear the pushback: *"We can't say or do anything anymore, everyone is just so goddamn sensitive, we can't do anything right, blah-blah-blah."* Groups in power are accustomed to taking up space and this familiarity enables an expectation that intentions alone are good enough—what follows therefore is a chronic dismissal of the impact that occurs. People are set-up to perpetually trespass the boundaries of others around them while seemingly having no awareness or ownership of the harm they're participating in due to the system's intentional design.

My brain and body were in conflict the moment he asked me for a hug—my brain intellectualized it was fine, my body resoundingly did not want to be touched and my nervous system perceived an awkward social interaction and potential misunderstanding if I handled it 'wrong'. My body therefore defaulted into a combined fawn and freeze response—neither of which *is* wrong, some of which is related to having experienced boundary violations and harm earlier in my life.

Given that the person who asked me for touch was cis, straight and male—and, as bell hooks teaches, 'possessing unawareness of his own identity and body's privilege and power' in the room, it's fair to say he was unaware of both my vulnerability and his power's visibility. Had he been more in tune with the ways in which power dynamics were present I believe he would've likely not asked for touch to begin with. Was it traumatizing? No. That doesn't mean that in the moment my body didn't still interpret it as a threat and engage in empty consent.

The experience was a reflective mirror of my own inner world and the ways in which empty consent still shows up within me. It also appeared as a mirror, reflecting back the parts within *him* he doesn't seemingly have access to. The more internal structure of self we have, the less we feel threatened or disrupted by others' boundaries. In fact, the more we anticipate others having or needing boundaries, the more safety we all access and the less risky denying others access to ourselves becomes.

Recently, a colleague I consult with reflected on an exercise we offer clients as a way of practicing awareness with embodied consent. On this particular day she'd practiced it in session with a male client. He'd sought her out to work on his relationship with his significant other which led into working on his childhood trauma.

We share similar approaches regarding how we intentionally assess and seek to honor client limits and capacity for trauma work. In this particular session he insisted he was ready for more, wanting to try something more targeted so she guided him into a therapeutic exercise we both practice with clients as a way of discerning how connected they are to their bodies and inner consent.

She asked him to close his eyes, take a breath and say aloud to himself the word '*no*'. This exercise can help clients connect to where they feel consent and boundaries in their body, it can invite connection to emotion or sensations internally as they say '*no*' or '*yes*' in a safe space. It's a way of practicing embodiment and attunement—it's also a way we can discern where we internally lack it. Memories may surface with the exercise that people choose to process in the session or contain for another time when they feel more ready. The exercise can help us notice places we feel resistant, hesitant, blocked or in need of more self-led permission and safety. It is meant to be practiced when we have capacity and feel open to incrementally being with ourselves and more specifically, be with our '*no*.'

When he tried the exercise he experienced a dissociative response that surprised both of them, defaulting to a frozen traumatized state. My colleague quickly and efficiently helped ground him to his surroundings and access self-care and agency. I am unable to discern how much his response was rooted in his particular story, trauma pattern and unique vulnerabilities, however what I *can* tell you is this–our society does not empower men to hear and honor their inner '*yes, no and maybe*' nor do we teach men how to hear and honor the '*yes, no and maybe*' responses of others.

Poet Floriano Martins writes "I protect myself by refusing to know myself". While perhaps not it's goal, patriarchy's primary tool *is* to disconnect men from themselves. The rules of patriarchy dictate that 'real men' ought to avoid their humanity while simultaneously socializing men to manage and deny the humanity of others. I will say it again: NO ONE WINS.

Mel Gentry Bosna

In a profoundly moving interview on the *Man Enough Podcast*, gender-nonconforming author, artist and public speaker Alok Vaid-Menon spoke these powerful words:

> *People have been taught to fear the very things that have the potential to set them free. The focus has been on comprehension, not compassion. What I tell men is that this is not about accepting trans and gender nonconforming people, this is about accepting yourself. If you do that work first, everything I'm going to say is going to make sense, but if you don't do that work, everything that I say is going to be inherited as an attack from a zero-sum ideology that makes you think that if other people thrive that you must somehow lose something? That's what's happening with misogyny in this country right now. I want to be able to walk outside without being spat on, I want to be able to live and not fear dying, I want to be able to wear what I'm wearing and not be called brave—and people are saying that's a threat? Darling, the threat is a system that has made you mistake your latent dissociation as a personality. That's the threat.*

Dismantling patriarchy is not an effort to erase men—quite contrary to that perceived threat, the vision behind dismantling this system is to more fully *honor men* as human beings deserving of the wide-breadth of emotional experiences humans can have. It's about inviting men to access an internal world they've been socialized to deny. Dismantling the system is about rebuilding a world where men access a more vibrant power within that isn't expressed as 'power-over' others, a world where men can feel safe enough within themselves to allow others to *also* exist fully as themselves.

A House Of Mirrors

Walking away from the patriarchal platform means walking down an alternative counter-culture path, one which allows men to more fully come alive as they return home to themselves, becoming more fully connected relationally too with others. A secure energy flows from this practice, one that empowers men to feel and be themselves with less threat–the losses involved with dismantling patriarchy are only to the system itself and the relational constraints where everyone inevitably loses if they stay and participate.

I want more for men than men have seemed to want for themselves. I recognize this now to be reflective of an embodiment and vulnerability many men haven't felt permission to experience. I want men to have more access to themselves because all of us, men included, are harmed when they aren't offered more vibrant options. Disembodiment and dissociation are the pillars to patriarchy and one of the primary systems that perpetuate empty consent.

Religious fundamentalism holds its own unique brand of patriarchal values and wouldn't be the powerful system that it is without them. Having your body and sexuality weaponized against you in the name of god however is a harm that *while* dependent on patriarchy also stands uniquely separate from it.

Religious Fundamentalism & Purity Culture

"As for me and my house, we will serve the Lord"

–Joshua 24:15, NIV Bible

Religion and spirituality can be both an individual as well as a collective experience that connects and restores us as we encounter what feels akin to divine power. It can deepen our relationship to ourselves, one another, and the earth we're learning to care more for and being cared for by. Some people name this as a higher power, I refer to it more often than not as 'source'.

Mel Gentry Bosna

This section is not referring to the beauty that spirituality and ritual can be, it's speaking instead to the ways in which the rigidity of religious fundamentalism hijacks consent development. I'd be hard pressed to tell anyone what to believe, who to worship or how to practice spirituality that otherwise connects them to restorative power, whether it be self or source. Due to the recurrence in my interviews and clients' experience which in many ways mirrored my own childhood, the fundamentalism of western Christianity's influence on consent development will be emphasized in the stories that follow.

Around the time I started this chapter I sent out a text to a few friends who'd either left formal religion or redefined their participation in it. I invited them to reflect on the following: define how patriarchy and religion have influenced your life. Do you feel an ongoing reverberation from either institution in ways you wish were less present or different?

One by one my friends' separate responses rolled in, my phone chiming with each of their replies. One particular response from a dear friend lit up my phone before immediately lighting up my body—Addison wrote, "*Both patriarchy and religion required me to shrink, dumb down, play small.*"

Addison was raised in rural Kentucky. She's always described herself as having a rather idealistic childhood, one where she roamed her neighborhood free, climbed trees, was encouraged to be messy and most of all felt happy. Her parents lived a creative life as homemakers and artists, they built a home where they seemingly had a lot of equity–so much so that despite having been raised in a rather conservative part of the southern United States, Addison didn't encounter the sharp edges of gender power dynamics until she left for college and found her way into a traditional evangelical bible church. This church is where she was given a stricter handbook than the bible, taught to be abstinent until marriage, celibate for life and submissive at all costs.

I sent Addison a follow-up text, asking if she felt she'd been promised anything specific if she played small in the ways that church was asking her. Moments later my phone lit up again with her reply.

"*I was promised protection. I could have certainty and security with getting my heart's desires–which turns out never happened. I was neither more safe nor did I ever find what my heart wanted.*"

A House Of Mirrors

I texted another reply, "Say more friend, if and when you have the capacity to share, no pressure." No one owes me their story or an answer to a text or my questions—this is one daily practice I use to affirm consent with my clients and friends—allowing for and reinforcing how permission and space exist for them to open up as well as withhold as they feel they need to.

My phone continued chiming, both Addison and other friends' responses flowing in. Perhaps unsurprising has been how eager people have seemed to *want* to be asked these types of questions, having not had enough safe places to share about their experiences—there's a longing to have our stories witnessed, our losses held.

The feeling that first lit up my body traveled to my throat, eventually sinking down into my stomach as I read Addison's next text message.

"I was literally shunned from the church I attended for over a decade because I started asking harder questions, which exposed the reality that I was actually only 'safe' as long as I was conforming to what I was being taught–as soon as I began wrestling with my beliefs and thinking for myself there wasn't room for me, my life didn't fit into the church's tiny box. I was single, childless and as I aged I was treated as a second class citizen. Despite the fact that I have always wanted to get married and start a family, and was in fact promised I would be given those things if I kept myself sexually pure, the outcome has been that I've ended up more alone now than any other season in my life."

Over the next few days Addison's words continued cycling through my body as I held them alongside dozens of interview transcriptions. The pattern of being asked to '*shrink, dumb down, play small*' in order to be seen as desirable by men, faithful to god and approved of by the church felt pervasive and recurrent in the interview transcripts. This pattern was woven throughout my childhood too.

I can't say playing small came very naturally for me due to the ways my particular trauma response developed–as a child I intuited it didn't seem to matter how much I *tried* to fit the mold of a submissive good-girl, my trauma pattern and personality's energy seemed to contrast those of the girls and women I was surrounded by, meaning I didn't seem as wired to *please*. I've observed some survivors fold into the fawn response of pleasing and codependency, both attachment wounds commonly derived from insecure and destabilizing relationships. I have zero judgment towards this response, in fact, I've often wondered why it wasn't *more* of my default response growing up. Other people perhaps would've responded more positively towards me albeit superficially if I had defaulted to people-pleasing instead of honing my defense mechanisms' edges.

The bite of my energy however often felt sharp, pointed, although I wouldn't say I acted in outright rebellion—it didn't feel emotionally safe enough to express myself so directly. If I wanted to be more or less safe I felt I'd have to be armored, bigger energetically than anyone else in the room, which I now recognize as a defensive posture that developed while quite young. Many of the people around me seemed chronically suspended between either disappearing within themselves or overpowering others, choosing a life of martyrdom or the reign of empire's narcissism. I consciously resented being asked to dull my edges and personality down–I did so when perceived to be necessary, when I needed to feel more safe but *god* did I resent being asked to be less of myself.

Many people grow up with a feeling of inadequacy, believing themselves to be 'not good enough.' It's reliably one of the more common core beliefs I encounter from clients in my office. Shortly following the belief of inadequacy is the message of being 'too much' to handle or love, a different variation of the same, old shame story. That belief is precisely what religion and patriarchy drone into me–I like my power and space *too much*, I have too much of a body, delighting in myself was dangerous and risky.

Reading Addison's words I was reminded of the internal resistance I'd felt in the church whenever asked simultaneously to be both less *and* more. When I asked what messages about being less/more people had received from their churches these words were most frequently used:

> BE LESS: opinionated, wild, noticeable, loud, curious, intellectual, willful, ambitious, emotional, sensual, permissive, assertive, outspoken, open-minded, sexual, questioning, independent, sexual, vocal, confident, prideful, sensitive, autonomous, confrontational, certain, armored, self-trusting, hungry, queer, powerful, less human.

A House Of Mirrors

> BE MORE: humble, quiet, pliable, homogeneous, trusting of god/leaders, committed, conforming, agreeable, grateful, sacrificial, gentle, modest, forgiving, patient, helpful, docile, dutiful, faithful, self-controlled, polite, contrite, dependent, feminine/masculine, pleasing, pure, obedient, easy-going, conforming, joyful in suffering, more willing to defer or be led.

The primary message many receive from Christian fundamentalism sounds like this: *Be less of yourself–less human–more like god. Do not lean on your own understanding but god's. The body is deceitful and untrustworthy, look to god. Listening to your body, needs, desires, intelligence and dreams are dangerous. Be less...you.*

Ironically, god seemed to sound a lot like, well, *men.*

Or at least the men I knew who held power.

When raised inside these communities during our formative years of development, we may find ourselves bridged between patriarchal and religious systems requiring our self-abandonment in order to meet needs for belonging and worth. We are conditioned to silence our intuition and ignore our personhood, faced with making decisions without valid alternatives: will we submit and belong to god and family, even if it costs us our humanity, or will we forsake what we know and audaciously choose ourselves for the possibility of belonging elsewhere as ourselves—outrageous considering how many of us are conditioned to see anything outside of this belief system as risking eternal torture.

Even if we leave these spaces we may encounter layers of exiled memories, wounds and pain from practices of self-abandonment that were contained within the body. Self-doubt is a foundational part of fundamentalist communities—the doctrines and relationships purposefully socialize humans to disconnect from their inner compass which is what's needed to develop self-trust.

The aftershocks of being required to submit to both god and men, ironically —*by both god and men*, may have lasting impact on our identity, sexuality and recovery.

We may feel those former requests tangled around our neck, choking the life out of our inner being and desires. A common lament I hear from those who grew up in toxic ideology is grief from missing out on who they could've become and how or who they could've trusted sooner had they not been silenced and withheld from knowing and trusting their intuition.

We were told it was a deceptively dangerous serpent who would suffocate our goodness, that only a feminine power would foolishly surrender to it. I now recognize it as a lie of cowardice, rooted in misogyny, substituted in lieu of being offered an alternative way–a third way, an honest way, dare I say, *a holy way into our fullness*. All systems of power and corruption rely on the absence of consent and the silencing of both our inner *and* outer voice, which is why many of us are taught emotions and bodies are bad, untrustworthy and necessary to distance ourselves from.

If playing small and submitting are the only ways to get our needs met, how could we *choose* any alternative path for ourselves without disruptive consequences like the ostracization Addison experienced? What was presented was a transaction–we could sacrifice our core sense of self in order that we might hopefully belong, or we could ask hard questions of the system, choosing ourselves while potentially facing abandonment by our entire community. This feels exceptionally painful when religion and god are used simultaneously as sifting agents to see what remains dare we desire and allow ourselves more.

I explored this with research participants in the first section of the interview and their responses consistently mirrored this inner conflict. After asking about the types of relationship options that were presented growing up (marriage, divorce, singleness by conscious choice, same-sex relationships, inter-racial relationships, etc.) and what they remember learning about consent (if they learned anything at all), I asked if participants were familiar with purity culture and comfortable sharing any thoughts or experiences they'd had with it. Given that the study spanned a large part of the United States and participants' backgrounds were diverse and unique from one another, I was surprised that the majority of participants were not only aware of purity culture but had been directly impacted by it.

In 2018 Emily Joy Allison coined the hashtag #ChurchToo in the wake of the broader social conversation Tarana Burke and #MeToo were making. Allison's intent with #ChurchToo was to identify the specific ways in which the Christian evangelical church participates in upholding toxic beliefs about sex, gender and sexuality in addition to directly protecting perpetrators that directly harm vulnerable people inside of faith communities. She writes, *"purity culture is the spiritual corollary of rape culture, created in Christian environments by theologians that teach complete sexual abstinence until legal, monogamous marriage between a cisgender, heterosexual man and a cisgender, heterosexual woman for life—or else."*

Or else.

Those two little words paired together have less invitational tone than 'say more', there's an ominous, threatening energy we all recognize when we hear them directed towards us. For those outside of fundamentalist communities it may not seem like much of a threat to buck the system of religion, I can see the casual shoulder shrug in my memory of someone who said, *"So what if you believe something different than your friends and family? Can't you just agree to disagree?"* However for those of us raised in rigid religious systems our sense of belonging, safety and at times, even our livelihood were entangled within conformity—there was neither room nor permission to disagree.

The majority of participants interviewed who had been exposed to religious fundamentalism also described a family system that was actively involved in church, again reminding me of my own childhood–rebelling against the doctrine would've meant not only probable rejection by community but the potential loss of family relationships as well. This was the case for about a quarter of the people I interviewed and also something I directly witnessed growing up while sitting in my own church's pew.

Mel Gentry Bosna

My fourth interview took place curled up inside the basement of a home in the Pacific Northwest. It was fall, rainy and the two of us curled up with plush blankets and mugs of hot tea to go over the questions. My mug was white and pink with a playful sketch of a woman's breasts on it. This conversation was with my friend Janie, a human I adore and whose childhood I had some knowledge of but realized shortly into the interview held significantly more pain than I'd previously been aware of.

Janie attended several different churches while growing up in the Southwestern United States, saying that at one point her family was involved with a cult. She and I had met around the age of eighteen at a church's college group event. It was a brief period of time we both tried to make church work for us, which in hindsight might've been part of what drew us towards each other, creating space for a friendship to develop.

Janie described her childhood family system as chaotic—disorganized at best, more often than not verbally and emotionally volatile. Her parents weren't together for long due to the toxicity of their relationship but the memories she has of them together involve a controlling father.

"He and my mom would walk into the grocery store and he'd grab her arm, tell her what she was allowed to buy–make it really clear, you know, he was the man of the house."

Janie spent more time with her mother, a woman who was very religious, emotionally and verbally abusive and, heartbreakingly enough, parented in such a way that Janie spent her childhood feeling hated by her.

Janie first became aware she was attracted to girls when she was in high school, describing her first love affair happening with a close friend. However despite her strong feelings, attraction to the same sex and the secret relationship that followed, it didn't occur to Janie she was gay as she had never seen representation of feminine lesbians in the world she grew up in.

"I had a relationship with my best friend. We were seventeen...I was in love with her and that's when I became consciously aware that I was attracted to women. Throughout my life I always pictured myself in a female relationship–it's weird to say and hard to believe now but it literally never occurred to me that I was gay. Like...I just never put it together which sounds both bizarre and obvious."

A House Of Mirrors

That relationship ended and she moved on, began dating men, assuming she'd get married, have children, raise them in the traditional family like the ones she'd seen modeled at church and on TV. There wasn't room to explore queerness as part of her identity or sexuality because, *"Being gay would've been a problem."*

I floated the question quietly. "Who would it have been a problem for?" The question seemed to hang in the air while the rain stretched her limbs down the window. The mug of tea I'd been gripping had gone from piping hot, to warm, to cool during the first section of the interview as my body held witness to the history Janie was sharing. I noticed her tone shifting, her voice breaking as she named what seemed to be an old story of shame regarding how long it took her to come out as gay to herself before she could eventually share it with others.

She momentarily detoured away from my question, instead pivoting into self-judgment. *"How could I not have known? I'd always pictured myself as a little old lady married to a woman at the end of my life. My first serious crush was with a girl–I was always attracted to women, how could I not have known I was gay until I was almost thirty? When I did finally come out, it wasn't like I was bisexual or questioning or anything either, like–I'm SUPER GAY."*

She and I were giggling as she described herself as the gayest of all the feminine lesbians in the world but I noticed tears were pooling in her eyes, how, despite our laughter there was a seeming heaviness weighing on her chest. While I sensed a lack of representation and overabundance with religious indoctrination were part of what had contributed to her sexual repression, I sensed a deeper wound had made it absolutely necessary for Janie to have concealed this part of herself from everyone, *including herself.* How could the timing and readiness been anything other than necessary?

I paused the recording, leaned forward, sat my cold tea down—was she open to hearing what I was experiencing as she expressed frustration and criticism surrounding how long it'd taken her to know and express these parts of herself. Her head hesitantly nodded, not so much from fear it seemed but from anticipation, both our eyes began tearing as I spoke words we often restrict when shame is present. I thanked the part of Janie that knew she was gay and did her best to hide it from the rest of her. I validated the wisdom and infinite goodness of this part of her that had kept her safe by hiding her full sexuality until she was actually safe enough to explore and express it—likely a very young, precious part that had discerned she wasn't safe enough yet to know–this part deserves recognition and gratitude.

This part likely repressed her sexuality because it understood what was at risk with knowing: "*Being gay would've been a problem.*" In Janie's case, part of her understood that because of her mother's religious, homophobic beliefs and the volatility that already existed in their home, being gay would have resulted in one more reason for her mother to react hatefully towards her. The human heart can only handle so much pain and life was already excruciatingly tender and hard. That part of Janie did her very best, tucking away as much as possible until years later when she'd left the Southwest, established boundaries with her family and forged her own way. She hid it from herself until she was safe enough to know, claim, live and welcome her sexuality and identity more fully home.

It was *pure joy* to bless this part of her that had helped her navigate childhood trauma–to honor with gratitude the ways she adapted in order to survive and how, despite such hardship she had found a way to herself nonetheless. She eventually left her family relationships for more reasons than this one, a choice she's allowed herself to make and maintain. Her healing includes grieving missed experiences with self-exploration during formative years of her life. However she can now see this self-repression was *absolutely necessary* for her survival and validate it should never have been necessary to begin with. If the world around her had been safer, the world inside her would've reflected that as well. The losses from her childhood live alongside the new ground she's taken as she more freely lives from her true self—it all belongs.

I see this pattern of inner burial repeated often in our stories. Many of us hide things that we don't feel not safe enough nor ready enough to be honest with ourselves about. People are often accused of being deceptive when the reality is that being truthful and vulnerable *can* come with a cost when our need for belonging is anchored to others' reactions towards us. So we repress our stories and memories deep within us, that is, if we can.

Elle and Marcus are two clients of mine who both grew up in rigid, religious homes. Elle knew she was bisexual around middle school, attending both a church and a school that were religious in addition to her family's beliefs and practices. She described a complete lack of sex education outside of abstinence-only information which led her to secretly search for information online as a young teen, desperate to try and learn more about what being bisexual meant.

A House Of Mirrors

Laughingly she told me about a time she literally broke the family's computer because of what her google searches turned up. Similar to my interview with Janie, we initially laughed about it before the heaviness surfaced as she remembered what her body experienced growing up feeling so very alone inside her family, school, and church–how very alone she'd felt in the world.

Marcus was raised in a family that attended a church that preached strict fundamentalism. He was home-schooled by his parents and creationism and abstinence were exclusionary parts of the curriculum he was taught. Similar to Elle, he knew he was gay from a young age and did everything possible to "convert" himself to becoming heterosexual. He tried to pray his gayness away and repented and fasted on his own behalf. His parents sought out conversion therapy for him through their church, everyone involved was certain that with faithfulness and time, he'd be different—and by different they meant 'straight'. He sat in my office recounting all the ways he knew he was gay, sighing heavily, *"Goddamn, I tried SO fucking hard not to be."*

Elle, Marcus and so many others I've supported have an additional layer of trauma they are working through–specifically the fear of burning in hell *because* of their queerness. Each of them processed specific memories of being told how much god despises queerness, seeing it—seeing them—as a perversion. The god they were raised with loves the sinner, hates the sin, which they were mostly told by people who 'loved them' enough to tell them this supposed truth. Friends and family who, unashamedly, preached that god hates homosexuality with such vitriol that the only way to be reconciled to this god would be to live a life of celibacy or be in a heterosexual relationship.

Despite their best and sincere efforts neither of them could reconcile nor exile their queerness away. They separately resigned themselves to having to walk away from the community and relationships, however this didn't mean that the fears instilled in them were left behind. Nightmares, flashbacks, and intrusive thoughts specific to burning in hell continue to occur for both of them despite having left religious systems years ago. Imagine being told how you were created was fundamentally wrong and then having to decide between living as yourself or serving a god who supposedly created and redeemed you at the expense of your self-rejection.

I can't tell you how many times I've sat in my office long after a client has left, processing my own grief at what religion has cost too many of us. The reality is that more often than not my clients who identify as queer and were raised in religious systems would have chosen to be straight *if it had actually been a choice*—in part because of the shame they'd been socialized to carry, in part because they wanted to belong to the families and communities who raised them, and, in part because who the fuck would actually risk eternal damnation because of an issue both as fundamental and as simple as sexual attraction? It does not make sense. Reducing it to a choice of lifestyle is ethically dishonest, spiritually incongruent and a privilege that comes from a position of power from heteronormative culture.

The answer is no one, *literally no one,* chooses these losses wholly and willingly. Loss, shame and pain are the consequences that follow having no other options with safe belonging. Similarly, I'd argue no one is actually choosing the god Christian fundamentalism serves when the risk of not serving him is significant loss and when the threat is eternal torture. Even when people do submit to this ideology it can only at best be a practice of empty consent if the underbelly is a threat to safety (whether in this life or the one after).

Fear and shame are emotional weapons used to manage behavior and they assuredly leave casualties in their wake–even among those who leave the system. There are ways people practice Christianity that do not use a heavy-handed god to control others. Many of my dearest friends identify as Christian and not a single one of them has tried to convert me, shame me nor present a god who is watching with a loaded gun inside his otherwise welcoming hands. If the religion you follow practices conditional belonging I'd beg you to explore how you're consenting and participating within it and at what costs.

Shay, a client I was so honored to support for a season, came out to their family as non-binary during the time we worked together. Similar to Ollie's experience shared in an earlier chapter, Shay encountered criticism and rejection from their parents. What was different from Ollie's experience was the specific language the rejection was embedded within. The words spoken to them were clear: not only was Shay unwelcome to come home for the holidays if they were wearing nail polish and using they/them pronouns, but to ask the family to accept how Shay was expressing themself would be the same as asking the family to dishonor god and enable Shay towards a life of destruction and sin. They would rather lose their relationship with Shay than to lose favor with the god they served.

A House Of Mirrors

The family felt as though Shay was backing *them* into a corner by being around Shay's self-expression—which ironically mirrors the experience many of us feel if we don't submit to the rules of patriarchy and religion. The 'choice' of either abandoning ourselves or be abandoned by others. Religious beliefs and personal identity however are not equitable in their vulnerability. In the same way cisgender men may struggle to see how power dynamics between men and women result in limits with consent equity, religious people may have difficulty recognizing how asking someone to deny their identity and needs for safety are neither equal nor equitable with having a personal or religious belief respected. People are entitled to develop their own thoughts, values and practices, be it political, moral or spiritual—no one however is entitled to oppress their beliefs onto others when it compromises needs for safety in this world.

Shay's request for their family to honor their boundaries and identity is not the same as the family's demands that Shay accommodate their belief system and emotional comfort. With an escalating rate of violence committed yearly against trans and non-binary individuals, one cannot argue the power of personal spiritual beliefs is remotely equal to actual lives lost. Until we all share the same fundamental rights and exist safely in the world *as ourselves*, we can assume consent and boundary practices are too often an expression of empty consent and one offered from a need for survival.

I have a foam baseball bat in my office I sometimes pull out when I have a client who is newly accessing anger and unsure how to express it. Hitting a mattress, couch or pillow with a foam bat or our fists can be one way we release emotion. Many of us who have been parented or governed by fear and shame may have anger lying dormant within us, waiting to emerge in a season we feel safe enough to access and express—for some of us that anger is directed towards our bodies or the parts of us that didn't 'fight back', a dismissal of the trauma response that purposefully helped us survive.

Anger is a purposeful emotion—when we get in touch with our anger we need appropriate ways to express it so it doesn't remain stored in the body nor result in coming out sideways in other problematic behaviors or vulnerable mental health issues that aren't in alignment with our values. Depression is often a symptom of repressed rage and grief that we perhaps don't know how to be with or often felt others react negatively too. Our bodies communicate to us, be it through our physical or mental health, emotional wounds which are held hostage within us that deserve care and relief.

85

Mel Gentry Bosna

In order to give ourselves more options to practice consent with, we must reckon with the fear and shame religious beliefs and patriarchy costs us. Shame isolates us from others, is often reinforced by others and without fail alienates us from ourselves and others. The specific comments Shay's family said to them are words I refuse to repeat, I will not participate in violence even in reference. However, I will tell you this—there were days after Elle, Marcus and Shay's therapy sessions where, once alone, I picked up the foam baseball bat in my office and released my own grief onto the leather couch. Days where as a mother, I wept over the words and actions their mothers had spoken over them, burying them with torrential pain in an effort to seemingly 'save' them from sin. No one wins when the options presented are abandonment of self, abandonment by family and community, abandonment by god. No one consents willingly to being harmed in this way.

Religious fundamentalism doesn't just target the sexuality and boundaries of the LGBTQ2+ community. Perhaps in less obvious ways but just as far-reaching it risks harm to all involved. In my interviews I spoke with cisgender, heterosexual men and women alike who felt shame about their bodies, desires, sexual drive and general needs. One participant described her parents' avoidance with her regarding sex education until her wedding day when her mother essentially burst into tears and told her "*it would eventually get better.*"

While her parents neglected talking with her about sex, consent and boundaries, the church youth group leaders did not hesitate. One of many metaphors she was offered about premarital sex equated her body with being a used, chewed-up piece of gum–essentially if she were to have sex before marriage all she'd be offering her husband later in life was something used and discarded. Hold those church messages next to the one her mother gave her: wait to have sex so you don't feel used, wait so the right man will want you, wait and even then, tears and a promise, *"it'll still hurt but eventually it'll get better"*. The amount of attention given to protecting purity, misassigning power and dismissing the actual experience and need for pleasure present a recurring set-up for those raised in purity culture.

Men are often portrayed as powerless to their sex drive, a message offered to men and women alike, which becomes another vulnerable behavioral pattern that plays out in relationships. If men weren't in control of their sexual desire then women had to be—which essentially means women hold the responsibility of purity without having any real power. How women and girls act, what clothing they wear and how they conduct themselves in front of others all carries the burden of responsibility for purity and safety, which, uncoincidentally is a perfect prediction for victim blaming when harm befalls them.

I've thought often of this. The ways men's eyes lingered and tracked me around the church, the leers experienced at a number of family gatherings, the ways girls were talked to as though we were older and more available than young adolescents should be. The default assumption was that because church and family were supposed to be safe that they therefore were, and that support would've been accessible if and when it wasn't safe, which it was more often not.

Even on the Sundays I walked down the aisle and collapsed at the church's altar for prayer when I actively no longer wanted to be alive, I still felt eyes boring on my body and found myself wondering how I looked kneeling down. I felt a gut-punching resentment while wondering if the dirty bottoms of my shoes were visible with the way I was kneeling, found myself silently hoping the outline of my underwear wasn't obvious to the hundreds of people in pews behind me.

I went up for prayer because I felt desperate and alone. Looking back now I can see how prayer was one of the only options I was presented with to try and alleviate my pain. Had therapy, medication and support from safe people been offered, would I have actually resorted to publicly kneeling? Growing up being watched and lusted over is an activation that shouldn't occur in any young person's body, an experience I know is universal to many and present both within and outside of religious spaces. Despite its universal commonality, the reality is that I experienced more objectification inside my church community and family system than anywhere else growing up and I wasn't even considered the 'pretty one' in my family or peer groups. It didn't matter, I was a girl—I had a body, it was as a problem.

Many of the men raised in purity culture whom I spoke with described varying messages they received surrounding sexuality and consent, primarily that they too should avoid temptation at all costs since their sex drives were uncontrollable and would lead them to harming others and engaging in sin. More than one of them described the shame of feeling that men were seen as monsters—their sexuality was out of control, wild, scary, displeasing to god. Like all others, their bodies too could not be trusted. This confusingly enough, was juxtaposed with messaging about women's bodies as being the ultimate thing to avoid as women were regarded as fragile, corruptible, yet somehow also to blame should men fall into the temptation of lust.

The expectation simply enough was this: do what you must to avoid others' bodies, avoid your own body and do this indefinitely because bodies are dangerous.

This belief exists in direct opposition to being a safe, embodied, consenting human being. Being connected to our bodies is absolutely essential to accessing our intuition and in order to practice consent consistently with ourselves and others. Bodies are not what's dangerous to relationships, sexuality and desire are not parts of ourselves to avoid and silence—what is potentially dangerous for our communities is for people to lack connection and understanding with how to safely honor, express and steward our bodies and desires in a way that's in alignment.

I could die on this hill but instead will shout it from a mountain: We cannot practice a reciprocal, vibrant consent with *anyone* without connection to our own body; purity culture neither prevents boundary violations nor protect us from harm because our bodies are neither the solution nor are they the problem as to why boundaries are trespassed.

Bodies and sexuality themselves are not dangerous, it's a lack of personal agency and relational understanding about boundaries and consent that creates vulnerability. It bears repeating: sexuality and desire are not the cause of boundary violations—disembodiment, entitlement and emotional dysregulation are, from my perspective, the primary factors contributing to relational harm.

Adolescence is already hard enough to navigate—the internal conflict of feeling bad about oneself, rejection of the body as out of control and the displacement of power onto the female body as the terrain of temptation is an experience more often than not wrought with confusion and guilt. Many participants described their questions and experiences as having been too embarrassing to have talked with anyone about.

A culture that perpetuates powerlessness and shame is also one that cannot clearly examine the *actual* power dynamics being expressed. Who holds the power and who is the power being held over? Additionally, due to the rigidity surrounding sex within fundamentalism, namely being abstinent until marriage or celibate for life, purity culture cannot address the foundational practices that must exist to ensure health in all our relationships: boundaries and consent.

Boundaries are the expression of consent. If consent is my body and intuition's collaborative inner '*yes, no and maybe,*' a boundary is the outward expression of consent. It is what is communicated externally to others about our inner world. A boundary without an embodiment practice is vulnerable to either being too rigid, lacking vulnerability and interdependence, or too permeable where we fold quickly when others dismiss or trespass on our boundaries.

Religious fundamentalism and purity culture uphold self-abandonment practices as those raised within it are taught to over-value the needs of others and to default to the laws of god: self-sacrifice as an expectation, conditioning people to delay some needs while denying others. Even necessary boundaries may be discouraged in an effort to encourage self-sacrifice and humility.

The most effective way to practice abstinence from my perspective would be to teach it as one of many options available, understanding that a '*no*' response holds power only if a '*yes*' response feels alive and accessible. A boundary set out of obligation, fear or shame is still a boundary, however its one expressed from a lack of safety not from the fullness of self. Informed consent includes comprehensive information about bodies, sexuality, relationships, safety, consent, boundaries, and potential risks and benefits involved without coercion from whoever is providing the information.

When information and options are offered to us in spaces we genuinely feel we are safe and belong, we are able to integrate the information alongside our personal values and ethics, able to explore the ever-evolving energy of our inner world's '*yes, no and maybe*'. I wholeheartedly believe this approach would reduce shame, sexual violations, unplanned pregnancies and abortions due to the increased safety that comes from honoring each other.

It's never been our wildness that's been a threat but the inability to embrace and steward our erotic energy in ways that mirror core alignment. Purity culture reflects the rigidity of all/nothing, black/white dualistic thinking and therefore dismisses our humanity by reducing us solely to our sexuality and options surrounding it.

Mel Gentry Bosna

Choosing sexual ethics that align with our deepest integrity without a cloak of shame, confusion, self-righteousness or dread leads to loving ourselves and others well, richly, wholly and safely. I want this for you. I want self-alignment and exuberant, unashamed, joyful self-expression for us all. I trust that if we had our basic needs met and more safe spaces to practice belonging within, there would be less harm.

People could *choose* what's in alignment from a place of inner calm: abstinence, monogamy, celibacy, polyamory, all or none of the above. Choose, from a different energy than fear and obligation, from an inner knowing having been offered other viable options to choose from. I am neither for or against the decisions people make regarding whether they wait until marriage to have sex, have open or closed relationships, participate in religion or atheism or the millions of alternative options that exist among those. What I *am* for is the robust, embodied practice of weighing and sifting through options that align with our values, affirm our integrity and support living with less fear, shame and threat. I want you to honor your body and beliefs in such a way that your inner compass guides you clearly and consistently into a deeper and fuller expression of yourself—and, I want you making room for others to experience this too.

I wrestled with what to include regarding my family's history as it isn't solely my story to share–this is a book about consent and boundaries after all. Sharing the experiences of clients and research participants whom I have the freedom to protect by changing names and details regarding identifying information is not the same as sharing about the family I grew up in nor the specific ways things have played out in my own marriage.

There's a greater risk involved with disclosing details about my personal relationships, it is after all, only *my* version of the story and lacks anonymity and inclusion of my family's perspective. Yet withholding it feels energetically out of alignment—I don't find it possible to write about the power dynamics of patriarchy and Christian fundamentalism without also including my family's shared experience with publicly navigating it.

Here is where I've landed: purity culture creates vulnerabilities that often mirror the same dissociated, shame messages of the broader patriarchal culture. We are humans with needs, bodies and narratives that we're trying to reconcile without always having the resources, skills and support to do so well. Religion often perpetuates a doctrine of self-abandonment and neither my parents nor I were spared this experience.

My parents were young when they married, having dated and been engaged a total of twelve weeks. Like many young people trying to stay sexually pure, they married quickly in an attempt to honor god and each other. I have always known them to have genuine and earnest intentions to love and serve others well, however they were socialized to neglect their own needs, which over time, led them away from themselves and each other. Later when their marriage very publicly fell apart it caused a disruption that was felt and judged by many since my father was employed by a large church. The reasons for our family crisis were layered and complex, one of which involved an affair my father had with a woman who was part of the church's congregation.

It's interesting looking back on that season of our lives, feeling both compassion towards my parents alongside an evolved perspective that's developed from both my feminism and personal healing journey, neither of which I had earlier on. I was a twenty-four year old social work student, two months into my brand-new-baby-marriage when the news of the affair surfaced and my father became unemployed. I was overwhelmed and defaulted to a familiar, family role of rescuing, rushing into forgiveness in an effort to salvage what little seemed left. It wasn't until years later I began to access more curiosity around what happened, the parties involved and those of us most impacted. The reasons for the infidelity are not mine to share in the same way I aim to be careful with how I speak of anyone's story.

However, I will say this—I can now see more clearly the ways I was socialized by my religious upbringing to protect my father's powerlessness and fragility when he was broken and repentant, so clearly *human*, while simultaneously socialized to default to his power and leadership when it came to my own vulnerabilities and needs. I had been conditioned to assume my mother would support him no matter the costs involved while also seeing the other woman involved as exclusively a Jezebel-character-of-sorts who had meant my father and family harm.

It wasn't until many years later I was able to confront how regardless of this woman's intentions and participation in the affair, my father was nonetheless one of her spiritual leaders which is a power differential. The social movements

Mel Gentry Bosna

#MeToo and #ChurchToo have stimulated more constructive and transparent public discourse in recent years in ways which have afforded me more clarity on how patriarchy and religion are deeply embedded in my own family system and relationships.

I have deep empathy and understanding for my father and the ways in which his self-abandonment played out, while also refusing to look away from the ways he participated in harm and abused his power. My compassion and conviction *can* and *must* be present together, accountability and vulnerability are love languages when practiced from healing, which is why I've included parts of our family story here.

Naively, inaccurately and most of all grievously I now understand what I couldn't discern then, which is how apt we are to violate the boundaries of others when we abandon our own needs and values. We cannot practice consent from a place of embodiment when we've compartmentalized and sought to silence whatever is occurring inside us. My father left himself, betraying his own values before he betrayed the relationship he had with my mother. I can speculate that may be true of the other woman involved as well. I can see this pattern play out in many other peoples' lives including layers of it in my own marriage.

A frequent experience specific to betrayal trauma is the feeling of having been harmed by someone you've chosen to love and be in a relationship with, be it infidelity, feeling stabbed in the back by a trusted friend, business partner or a seemingly-random-act of violence somewhere you'd previously felt safe—a particular type of shame is experienced when harm happens in a way we feel blindsided by. Anytime we participate in self-abandonment whether conscious or not, we can anticipate it will lead to an erosion of our values and boundaries. Similarly, when we experience abandonment in a relationship with others it not only erodes relational trust but can impact our sense of self-trust as well as we wrestle with the question, "*How could I have let that person in, how could I have let that happen?*"

I've processed this specific wave of grief and shock with clients and friends. I have felt the long-lasting reverberations of it in my own life too—the experience of surveying the aftermath of harm done without your consent and the following process of discerning whether or not a relationship and life are worth trying to rebuild. It's tempting to become hyper-focused on the ways we've felt

A House Of Mirrors

abandoned, we may have difficulty seeing how the person who harmed us likely did so out of their own abandonment and self-betrayal.

The invitation to either abandon or align with ourselves is present when harm is happening, it remains present as we sift through and reclaim our bodies and stories. Whether we run, stay, destroy or rebuild relationships, moving forward has everything to do with how much of ourselves and bodies we can be with while embracing the tenderness of our pain. It's from this embodied space we can access consent rather than simply react to our wounds and needs.

I am no one's judge, which includes my parents.

I needn't know or understand the entirety of their story to feel confident that it was at least partially shaped by the roles a broader patriarchal, heteronormative culture offered them of man and woman alongside the church's expectations to be good, pure and self-sacrificing. I don't doubt both my parents felt powerless in different ways and at different times, both were harmed by the fall-out of what happened after the affair, and, the impact of the trauma and their options moving forward were neither equitable nor fair.

I often wonder if my parents would have consented to another path for their lives had they experienced alternative options along the way. I can imagine there having been seasons it would have mattered to have felt like they had more options—not because they're unhappy now, they're not. They've steadily, sweetly found their way back towards themselves and each other despite years of loss and heartache. I am proud of them, moved by their commitment to build a new life. Nonetheless, would they have chosen something different if so much hadn't been expected of them to begin with, if they hadn't been isolated and ashamed as they navigated a public scandal and career loss?

What would I have chosen for myself had I experienced more emotional safety, permission and space to be an angry, angsty young adult through one of many family disruptions? Perhaps most importantly—what would it have all looked like if there had been paths to consent along the way, prior to the feeling of pain and public shame backing us into a corner. If we were taught how to listen to ourselves and honor our bodies, allowed to change our minds while staying within our integrity and boundaries—how much wreckage could we have avoided, or better yet, how many places of sweet sanctuary could have been built instead, churches included?

Mel Gentry Bosna

Purity culture offered me very little regarding my sexuality, instead it anchored me into a limiting and power-shaping heteronormative belief about my body: that is to say I was taught bodies were *dangerous* because of what men's bodies desire and what women's bodies possess.

I was taught my body was a site for trespassing, meaning if I was not careful male desire for it was going to become a problem. Careful was aptly substituted for modest—if I were to remain pure, which equated to safe, it meant I must guard mine and others' abstinence. I ought to erase any means for desire to exist, both mine, although it was never explicitly talked about, and more importantly male desire, which was centered, throned, feared and marveled at.

When I think back to my early years of puberty, I feel aghast at the responsibility my eleven year old body carried to keep my own desire from budding and adult male desire in check. It feels similar to willing a ripe piece of fruit from falling from a tree's branch except I was no gardener, just a child trying not to bloom.

In the same breath that I was told not to have a body desirable to men, I was socialized to prioritize having the kind of body that *was* admirable to everyone else. A body that was feminine, curvy, small, demure, that wasn't scarred or different. A body men and women alike both approved of, coveted but not lusted after. Everything felt anchored to my body and if purity culture taught me anything, it most of all reinforced I had to both deny and control this body that men wanted and women criticized. No matter how I tried to diet, purge, drug, ignore or dress myself up, my body didn't appear, perform or adapt the ways I was taught it was supposed to by white, heteronormative church culture. I seemed to be fucked.

Perhaps most impactful, religion shaped an understanding that my body was not my own. In addition to men being corrupted by it, I was told that god had to redeem the brokenness of my body through the breaking of Christ's body. Bodies become places we defame and others trespass which leads many of us to regard our body as the home we either abandon, desecrate, decorate or protect. I learned this as a toddler, a first grader, at eleven, fifteen and every year in some repeated capacity as people have treated my boundaries one way or another.

A House Of Mirrors

Religion taught me that my body was never intended to be my own and that any urge, desire, emotion or need that arose from my body was untrustworthy.

This was reinforced for me at church and home. I dieted with my mother, listened to my father comment on the bodies of others, watched my sister's body disappear through restriction, eventually resigned myself that I'd have to be good at other things *besides* having a body. I couldn't seem to beat mine into submission and my resentment about being asked to exist other than how my body seemed wired only grew. I think back to how much more gentle a transition into adolescence I could've experienced if I'd had safe spaces for my body and desire to occupy. I likely wouldn't have felt the same pressure to diminish myself nor felt exploited by others.

I experienced this the weekend I learned about my father's affair. Freshly married, I parked my husband's turquoise truck around the corner from my parents' home per my mother's request so my father wouldn't be deterred from coming inside. They eventually disclosed to me what was happening, I offered words of forgiveness as a default response without having time to process what I was feeling.

The emotional aftershock reverberated through our family a week later as we sat together in a pew in the front of the sanctuary. A special meeting had been organized, the entire church had been invited and the matter of discipline was being discussed. I sat there with my arm around my dad's shoulders and as the church filled up, my body filled herself up too with what I now recognize as anxiety and dread. I know what it feels like to have hundreds of eyes bored into the back of your family's heads because of what a man's 'unmastered desire' and body could do.

I can still feel how the energy rose and fell as he walked on stage and confessed. Seeing a person you're supposed to depend on cry in front of hundreds of people is a wave of disruption I hope I never feel again. It took me years to imagine what my mother felt that day as I'd been socialized my whole life to over-value male fragility and defer to male leadership and power. It took me decades longer to imagine what the woman involved in the affair felt about her own story and body.

I've stopped imagining, instead, I've come home to my body whom I lovingly now refer to by name and with pronouns: she remembers and will tell me—she was there, she lived it. Religion and purity culture did their damn best to divorce me from her, to convince me she belonged to others, that I couldn't listen or trust her.

Another reason consent feels impossible to practice inside of fundamentalism is that in order *to* consent our bodies would first need to be recognized as our own. We must be seen by others and also see ourselves as having an innate wisdom, which in turn would empower us to listen to our body, discern our desires, weigh them against our values and trust our inner compass' direction. Personal sovereignty is *incompatible* with all forms of fundamentalism and no one can practice consent without having sovereignty over their lives and bodies.

The closest experience I have now to holiness happens inside vulnerable conversations. The opportunity to be a living, breathing, human mirror is a covenant I practice with those of us who survived religious trauma and intend to save our lives from it. Getting to speak with clarity and certainty to the parts that survived these painful systems is a sacred privilege I hope I never take for granted.

There is room for all of us to belong and have a seat at the table. Patriarchy and religious fundamentalism would deny so many of us inclusion while demanding we be grateful for the opportunity to serve those seated. I want more for you, for our collective spiritual practices, for the world as a whole.

Any system or person that requires us to "*shrink, dumb down and play small*" is operating from authority that derives itself from a 'power-over' model. Empty consent will be glorified and required, all while leading us to an overflowing tomb. *We can and must say no to these demands.*

Increasingly, many of us are exploring how pain and uncertainty might be processed and released as we pursue an alternative third-way path from the dominant ones we're offered culturally. More of us are rejecting the old binary of having to choose between abandoning ourselves or being abandoned by others. It's possible to find a path of reclamation where we discover new ground, leading us to our chosen family and community. Never without loss but with a determination to *live* and to do so less alone, relentlessly aligned with our integrity.

A House Of Mirrors

Below is an excerpt from a longer poem my dear friend, writer and energy worker Stephanie Greene wrote. It currently hangs on one of my office walls, above my desk where people frequently stop to take it in:

> *And it all comes down to this*
> *A gospel written in the living*
> *An incantation we pass hand to hand,*
> *Soul to soul*
> *It's this—if you do nothing else but run,*
> *Run in the direction of you*

It can feel heartbreaking, physically excruciating to bear witness to the stories included in this section. It's been no small feat to claim and recover my own. If you are reading this and perhaps entrenched in a religious doctrine that asks you to abandon yourself or reject others in order to belong, I beg you to reconsider any human or system 'protecting' you by disconnecting you *from you*, perhaps demanding you become smaller still.

Parts of you may also be participating in your smallness—intending your safety, working on your behalf, likely restricting you from being the fullest version of yourself in the process because they haven't yet discovered another way. It's possible though—to live a life where you trust the goodness inside you, where you forgive the many ways you've left yourself over and over again in an effort to secure the love and acceptance of others. It's possible to let love in without being harmed so greatly in the process.

I'd audaciously claim that it's even possible to forgive and love the specific areas of your heart that cracked each time you abandoned yourself in an effort to secure the love and acceptance from god himself. Your heart and body may ache even now. I understand why, and also understand what it's cost you to try and be good all the time. However I cannot end this section in good conscience without pleading with you, sister-wife-brother-friend, please hear me out: a richer, safer, sweeter life with or without the divine of your past remains. Come, away from the stone altars you've been asked to kneel at, come towards home, return to you. You do not have to be perfect nor pure to have a seat at this table, you can show up as you, choose you, be human too.

Mel Gentry Bosna

I've watched Elle, Marcus, Shay and dozens more reclaim their paths from the religious fundamentalism they were raised inside, determined that despite the costs involved they could and must save their lives. I've watched Addison and Janie forge new ways for themselves too, living more wildly and freely as their fuller selves felt safe enough to emerge.

I want this for them and deeply want this for you too.

How does this tie into consent? I'll tell you–the more of you that returns home, the more embodied and full of yourself you become, the more access you'll in turn have to what's happening inside you with specificity to your needs and desires. The more attuned you become with yourself, the more discerning you'll become with others' energy and boundaries as well. We are safer for *everyone* when we belong to ourselves, brimming with our truest selves, when we're awake.

Musical artist Maddie Zham's lyrics from her song "If It's Not God" come to mind now, the unique edges of her voice soften during the chorus as she sings:

> *Something inside me was always steering left*
> *What father picks a few just to leave the rest*
> *I heard a voice inside my head, they disagreed*
> *If it wasn't God, then thank God it was me*

Thank god it was you. You being you is always a good thing.

White Supremacy

"The master's tools will never dismantle the master's house."

–Audre Lorde

A House Of Mirrors

This section is not meant to be one that chronicles United States' history as better books have been written by experts and authors whose voices are more relevant than mine–my opinion is not one that needs to be centered nor amplified on this subject. However, to exclude white supremacy from the conversation on consent and the ways in which it continues to disrupt access and practices of it today would be negligent on my part, and a direct participation of harm.

Note in this section that I use the words *bodies of culture* in place of, or in addition to, people of color, which is more commonly used as a descriptor when white people write about anti-racism and white supremacy. Therapist and somatic abolitionist, Resmaa Menakem, introduced me to this language. His books and website expand on this shift: "*I speak of bodies of culture to refer to all human bodies not considered white....This both acknowledges our existence as human bodies and displaces the other terms that make white bodies into the norm and otherize everyone else.*" Somatic abolitionism centers the body's value, inherent worth, trustworthiness and wisdom.

As a white woman whose European ancestors participated in violent colonization of this continent, I do not ever get to claim expertise on or act as a spokesperson for bodies of culture, nor can I claim understanding of nor determine the needs that any individual or community has. To do so would be ongoing participation in controlling the narrative, restricting body autonomy, gaslighting others' sovereignty and violating consent.

My commitment in this chapter is to name what belongs to *my history* and *my body* and the ways I am learning to recognize white supremacy inside of me— reckoning with how I see this system violate consent, mine *and* others. I will undoubtedly do this imperfectly and reflect differently about it as I own, decolonize and reclaim more of myself in the years to come. I commit as best as I can discern to stay in my lane.

There is a list of resources specifically curated for those in white presenting and identifying bodies on my website and in the appendix of this book. Also and forever: pay Black women for their labor, support and protect Black joy.

White supremacy systematically and pervasively hijacks consent development and practices. The history of the United States is saturated with evidence regarding ways in which white bodies have violated the consent and boundaries of bodies of culture broadly and Black and Indigenous humans most specifically for the purpose of expansion and maintenance of white power and control over resources.

It's absolutely relevant for white bodied people in the United States to name and own the ways in which white supremacy has historically violated the consent of entire nations, communities, families and individuals. The following only being a few examples: the colonization of land belonging to First Nation Indigenous peoples, the cross-Atlantic African slave trade which established and sustained a violent system of chattel slavery, Japanese internment camps, Jim Crow segregation, the prison industrial complex, the separation of families at the US/ Mexican border and so, *so* many more.

Previously I've highlighted systems of power I've personally been harmed by however as a white woman I am in a position of power which means I am more vulnerable to violate the consent and boundaries of bodies of culture because of my internalized white supremacy. I do not have to *feel* powerful to possess and abuse my power—I do not have to *feel* aware of my fragility to react to it either.

This does not mean that I'm unharmed by white supremacy. In fact, we all are harmed, no one is exempt from the system's violence. Similar to the ways men are harmed by patriarchy, white bodied people are harmed by white supremacy too. However and this point ought to be the clearest thing outlined in this book— the harm I experience from whiteness is not remotely equitable to what bodies of culture experience from whiteness. It is necessary for me to see both the ways that whiteness harms and protects me as a white bodied woman—necessary, as it is my responsibility to steward, transform and hold myself accountable to.

In the same way cisgender, heterosexual men are not always conscious of their impact on others due to the power their bodies and identities occupy, white people may not always be cognitive of their power—this is not an excuse. Whiteness is considered a default identity and purposefully made less visible to those who hold it. This is an intentional component with how race has been constructed by white supremacy.

In the section on patriarchy I included bell hooks' words and they are equally relevant to this section: "*Most men never think about patriarchy—what it means, how it is created and sustained.... Men who have heard and know the word usually associate it with women's liberation, with feminism, and therefore dismiss it as irrelevant to their own experiences."*

In the similar vein that most men don't regard patriarchy as anything other than a women's issue, most white people are unlikely to think of white supremacy and racial justice as issues relevant to anyone other than bodies of culture. Admittedly, it would rub me the wrong way to have a cisgender man write a book speaking on behalf of women or queer folks' experience. I'm more interested in witnessing the ways a cis man is exploring internalized patriarchy inside of *himself*. I want to hear how he's taking ownership and practicing accountability for his participation in this corrupt system, how he's repairing his relationship with his own emotions and body.

If we want to build a world for all humans to safely exist as themselves within, we must consider both the collective ways we dehumanize each other and the ways we individually participate in violating consent and boundaries. One such way white people can and *must* practice embodied consent is to be able to be with, own and repair the ways white supremacy lives in our stories and bodies, subsequently contributing to less safety for others and ourselves. Learning how to decentralize and destabilize white supremacy is part of building a consent culture.

I grew up with a cognitive understanding of race, much of which was understood and experienced within the context of my church's missionary work. The way I thought about race was that it was *outside* of me, which is how whiteness was centralized, the default baseline my worldview developed from.

My family participated in a number of short-term missionary trips in border towns in Mexico. When I was eleven I took my first flight to the continent of Africa where my father worked with local churches in Egypt. My involvement with short-term missionary work throughout my adolescence was with an inter-denominational evangelical organization, where I spent time in Latin America, Africa and Europe. I look back now on those experiences with a very different lens as my perspective on religion and colonization has significantly changed. I recognize now ways parts of me participated in harm even if other parts of me intended service. I see this specifically in the ways that white saviorism was present alongside the centering of my own culture inside of other cultures.

Mel Gentry Bosna

Even as I write these words I can feel the tension inside my body as I own the discrepancy white supremacy created inside my body. For example: taking pictures of children at orphanages without seeking consent and expecting others to speak English to me even though I was in their homeland. I would return to the United States and in the sharing I'd do about the trip, would center the poverty of the people I was exposed to and the work my team did—poverty and oppression, mind you, that was often a direct result of colonization. I can see now how focusing on the seeming relief missions brought to those communities and the gratitude expressed by the people served also upheld my worldview of white saviorism. I feel the presence of regret in my body now as I reflect on my participation—I don't want to avoid it nor become stuck in it, shame serves no one. Naming and repairing what belongs to me however is something for me to steward so I don't continue the same patterns.

As an adolescent I felt a sense of overall morality from doing this type of service. I now have enough shame resilience to be able to recognize the ways I felt a sense of superiority over other white people too. Missionary and volunteer work constructed a self-identity of being a *good* white person unlike the *other* white people I knew who were focused on their own ambitions and pleasure. I now understand this combination came from a blend of white supremacy and fundamentalism yet regret nonetheless my participation in short-term missions.

It wasn't until 2003 in my senior year of college that I was graciously called-in by two professors in back-to-back semesters. The first, a Black woman, held up a metaphorical mirror so I could see the fallacy of meritocracy, the belief that if people worked hard enough and were smart enough we'd all be able to achieve success, escape poverty and avoid hardship. I can't pinpoint specifically how or where I learned this, which in turn leads me to believe it was simply reinforced *everywhere*. Consequently the belief of meritocracy allows us to think of success and safety as individual experiences of achievement and therefore individual experiences of failure when they don't happen—forms of victim blaming and gaslighting.

In a similar tone to how women are asked what they were wearing when they experience harassment and assault, it's also insinuated that if someone hasn't achieved financial success it's because they didn't work hard enough and therefore deserve whatever their plight may be. The whole 'pull yourself up by your bootstraps' fallacy, which of course denies the reality that a white bodied boot is likely standing on your neck. This particular professor challenged me in such a way that I began understand that while I was marginalized in the world as a woman, my body housed unearned privileges, power and resources due to other identities she holds.

This class and professor introduced me to intersectionality, a term Kimberlé Crenshaw coined in the 1990s and restated in a 2020 interview with the Times, explaining it as follows:

> These days, I start with what it's not, because there has been distortion. It's not identity politics on steroids. It is not a mechanism to turn white men into the new pariahs. It's basically a lens, a prism, for seeing the way in which various forms of inequality often operate together and exacerbate each other. We tend to talk about race inequality as separate from inequality based on gender, class, sexuality or immigrant status. What's often missing is how some people are subject to all of these, and the experience is not just the sum of its parts.

Prior to college I'd only considered issues related to equality, I hadn't considered the *compounded* vulnerabilities that exist due to inequity. White supremacy enabled me to see myself as beneficiary, Christian fundamentalism taught me there was morality to be found in service and submission, white capitalism promised if I worked hard enough that I would be inoculated from poverty and suffering. These systems and beliefs are embedded in our culture, which means they are also internalized inside us and transmitted through us.

The second professor, a white woman, drew lines more definitively and boldly around my internalized white body supremacy, something I now recognize she had more safety to do than my Black professor did. While it *is* the responsibility of white people to call each other in and hold each other to account, I see the ways in which white bodied fragility reacts to feedback coming from others as, well, less palatable—another discrepancy of the-so-called-equality that the United States claims.

This professor relentlessly redirected students in class conversations away from our default pattern of deflection albeit through individualism—every time a white student tried to bypass self-reflection and accountability with injustice and inequity she'd draw them back towards their and others' humanity and participation. The takeaway that imprinted on my body and beliefs was the deconstruction of meritocracy's underbelly: white people wanted societal privilege without responsibility, the benefits of a kingdom without blood stained walls and we wanted it in such a way that we could uphold the belief that we somehow deserve it or earned it fair and square. This is a gross betrayal of the values the United States espouses and *should* break our hearts instead of breaking the bodies of those who either lost or forcibly built this country.

After that year I saw the world differently and more importantly, could see parts of myself more clearly. My options were to own and repair what belonged to me or hide the truth from myself, the latter of which would require the betrayal of my own integrity.

Nearly twenty years later I'm still practicing this self-excavation. I used to see it more directly in my behavior but I've begun to sink into what it feels like *inside my body*–the places where it seems more transformative change and obstruction is occurring and absolutely necessary. If all we ever do is focus on the symptoms of power, in this case racism, then at best we'll only be modifying our beliefs and behaviors. Perhaps this could decrease some margin of harm in the world however the root of all violation happens on a deeper, somatic level—inside our bodies.

This is always the truth with trauma—the origins and cause of harm as well as the impact of the harm are experienced somatically. Bodies are our homes which is why we cannot think our way to wellness, healing, racial justice or consent. Thinking is not the portal into where most of us access our needs and vulnerabilities. People cognitively understand consent and simultaneously violate it often for this *very* reason, what we know must be integrated and felt if we want to actually honor it in the moment.

I noticed this discrepancy in my body a few years ago at a meeting hosted at my office with other mental health professionals from the community. There were four white women present, myself included, and two other bodies of culture present, one man and one woman. To my knowledge we all identified as straight and cisgender. We passed around blueberry muffins, donut holes and joked about a million different things between exploring how we could provide better community mental health care. I don't remember exactly what was happening with the conversation as leading up to this particular moment the meeting had overall felt light, collaborative, benign—that is until one of the white women present used language that was racist.

It immediately reverberated in my body, I didn't just *know* it was inappropriate, *I felt it.*

Shocked, my eyes scanned the room as the conversation didn't stop–I began to second guess whether I'd heard her correctly. My eyes locked with my friend's, the only Black woman in the room and I knew with confirmation that the comment had been made, we both had heard her. My body simultaneously felt lit up while also feeling frozen—I couldn't seem to process quickly enough to *say* something, *do* something—as minutes passed I felt stuck with how to bring the conversation back to the comment since the group either hadn't noticed or was moving forward. I was immediately ashamed and upset with myself. I knew better, felt it all wrong and recognized I was not acting in alignment with my values. Even as a part of me was tangled up internally in a stress response, I felt stuck.

Eventually people left and I sat in my office staring at the window, interrogating the frozen parts of myself. It took some time for my body to settle and parts of me judged that too—I deeply regretted not responding differently, wanting to have been better, safer, kinder. I was concerned for my friend and ashamed of my silence. In order to find a way back to myself, I dropped into my breath which led me into my body, practiced curiosity towards the parts that I was tempted to reject. Engaging this skill helped me then and supports me now with turning towards the parts of me that, without conscious consent, are still drenched in white supremacy—these parts need transformation and I can't do this work by denying their existence. I had to find a way to sit with myself and face what had happened inside me and find a way back towards who I want to become so I can act accordingly.

At this point I felt tempted to rush towards an apology and somehow try and make things 'right', as though that option actually existed. Many of us wait too long to say or do something because of a belief that there's a perfect way to show up—one that doesn't involve us looking bad, getting it wrong or having to bear any consequences.

What I wanted was to have acted in alignment with my values and beliefs in the moment that harm happened—risked it being uncomfortable and awkward. Even if I later unpacked my frozen response surrounding why I couldn't seem to mobilize, I still feel deeply convicted that I didn't risk more of what was right in the actual moment harm had occurred. Redoing the past wasn't an option obviously, the moment had passed and I had to find a way back in order to realign my actions with who I wanted to be.

This involved reckoning with what had happened inside my body during the meeting. I didn't want to offer a performative apology nor one rushed from shame and anxiety—I've been given my fair share of generalized, blanketed apologies throughout my life that lacked insight and accountability.

Layla F. Saad, author of *White Supremacy & Me* writes, "*These are the ways that white supremacy is the water and not the shark,*" which I understand to mean that more often than not white people born in the United States continue to regard white supremacy as the KKK or perhaps overtly racist language and policies, rather than see it as the normalized, internalized experience happening within white bodies.

This often results in a failure to act when other groups are exploited, is what determines *whose* bodies are given the benefit of the doubt and is specifically how white women default into patterns of self-protection and uphold supremacy culture. The reality is my body is *almost always* given the benefit of the doubt in the world I live in and whiteness, especially white femininity, banks on my body's visibility, allowing white women to bypass responsibility and culpability.

Whiteness exists as a veil concealing power while simultaneously emphasizing white women's vulnerabilities. I can see the ways I've defaulted into this, that meeting included. I regret not saying anything the moment the comment was made. While it was important to explore what was happening *inside* my body and the parts that had participated in harm, I needed to have leaned into the messiness of imperfection and risked engagement *sooner* than I did. I needed to invite the other white people present into accountability sooner too.

A House Of Mirrors

During the meeting my fear of getting things wrong activated my body's stress response, making it difficult to call myself and the other white women into work that belonged to us. Please hear me: this is not an excuse, it is a part of me I alone am responsible for maturing. I consulted with four women of culture for feedback on this chapter and one offered this response regarding what she'd like to hear from more white folks in these situations:

"I am afraid that speaking up right now might in fact cause additional harm to (person of culture's name), so I apologize in advance if this comes out awkwardly. But I am choosing to take that risk because I cannot allow this moment to pass or this meeting to end without addressing the shift and the discomfort I felt when _____ was said. I think we need to talk about this or at least acknowledge what happened."

No one wants to be seen as the villain, especially when white culture over-values white peoples' motives—white supremacy is hyper-fixated on good intentions and in extreme denial of actual impact and harm. When we freeze in situations that deserve action, we adapt the story to exonerate ourselves from culpability—this is sometimes conscious and always self-protective. Our bodies react and often censor what needs to be seen, heard and changed about ourselves due to our avoidance of discomfort or fear of conflict.

I can reflect on this now with clarity only because I've been intentionally building shame resilience and practice recognizing the ways my fragility allows me ignorance with certain truths about myself. I see white women chronically dismiss their participation in harm too, seeing themselves as vulnerable, fragile and subsequently as the victim.

In psychological terms this is sometimes referred to as the Bystander Effect: the inaction of people in group situations who would otherwise *want to act* but are instead frozen as they witness an event or incident that violates their own values. Rather than respond in alignment people are silent, passive, seemingly paralyzed, hoping someone, *anyone* intervenes. In fact the more people present when something 'bad' is happening the less likely an individual is to help and act accordingly with their values.

As a clinician I recognize this as a freeze or fawn trauma response which I explore more in the next chapter. I have compassion for how our bodies struggle to navigate well situations that they interpret as unsafe or feel unequipped to handle, *and,* I can allow this understanding to coexist alongside deep frustration, shame and regret, especially given that what we perceive as unsafe may be an actual threat to others. Inaction often stems from internalized societal power along with feelings of powerlessness, inaction contributes to ongoing oppression of others as a lack of response results in diminished safety.

I can and must own how fear of criticism and anxiety surrounding engaging in anti-racist work the 'wrong way' were present in my passivity. This awareness didn't present itself immediately, it was only after reflection, internal interrogation and conversations I sought out with people willing to hold me accountable that I could discern the underbelly. My desire to distance myself from discomfort co-existed next to my insecurities around speaking up and getting it wrong. At the end of the day my silence wrapped in fear and shame contributed to a violation against my own values *and* more grievously to me, caused harm towards others in the room. It was violence experienced in a familiar and often minimized expression by white culture—white supremacy was activated inside my body, which happens inside peoples' bodies *all the fucking time.*

What followed the meeting were tender, imperfect and ongoing conversations. I reached out to my friend and the other body of culture who'd been present, owning my silence and participation in harm. The next day I followed up with the white woman who had made the comment in the meeting. My friend and I continue to explore my responsibility with leaning further into an imperfect practice moving forward. She does not owe me these conversations, her time, energy or friendship—however I owe her repair. It remains necessary for me to hold what we both felt that day: I betrayed her trust and my own values.

Contrary to how it may feel in our bodies, no one is destroyed or obliterated from discomfort. We may however, feel held hostage to discomfort through our avoidance of feeling it when we need to. When we prioritize feeling comfortable over being in alignment with our integrity we experience a recurrent erosion of trust with others and end up blocking our own growth and maturity from happening.

The natural consequence from being silent during that meeting was that the safety of my friendship was compromised. Due to a cultural value of perfectionism, people are afraid of criticism which is one reason the messiness of engagement is avoided. Instead of risking on behalf of their values, white bodies may cling to a fantasy that eventually they'll be ready, prepared and polished enough so as to avoid any uncomfortable experience that would result from doing or saying something 'wrong'.

Consent, boundaries and intimacy are neither fixed nor guaranteed and like all parts of a relationship we must proactively continue to lean in, engage and own what belong to us—safety is either being reinforced or eroded based on our willingness to risk for more collective safety rather than self-preservation.

We stare at the menu a full ten minutes longer than what others may consider reasonable, laughing about our shared indecisiveness. V, as her friends call her, settles on a few sides and half-orders so she can try multiple things. I ordered the "Bravocado toast" and a pineapple upside down pancake to share for dessert. We agree, breakfast any time of day is a good thing.

V is a friend and colleague and as we sit and eat our hearts out we explore ways our experiences overlap, a conversation that started in 2006 when we were in grad school and has evolved over the last many years. We share an upbringing that taught us to distrust ourselves and bodies. We were both raised in the Southwest, are women working in mental health, parenting kids around similar ages and raised in deeply religious family systems. We have a lot of common ground and parts of identity that are not shared, V is a woman of color and I am a white woman—a reality that may always bear some level of unsafety for her which I've been trying to feel and name so she doesn't have to.

We eat the pineapple bits out of the pancake since predictably they are the best part, I ask her "what are the ways you recognize white people haven't expected you to have boundaries or asked for your consent?"

V puts down her fork, "*SO MANY. I don't know if I could count them all!*"

I want to give her time to eat and reflect, trusting she'll share more if and when she wants to, she doesn't owe me this conversation.

"*I suppose the predominant pattern is just how centralized whiteness has always been. As an immigrant family, assimilating to be as white as possible has just*

109

always been the goal." She chews, shrugs her shoulders and continues, *"both white people and my family expected this from me."*

I sip my juice, notice the heaviness in my stomach, these conversations are important and almost always hold monumental loss. In an earlier season of my life a conversation like this would've held discomfort for me and I would've been prone to react self-protectively—it's why so many white women avoid having them, it's also what makes us unsafe to have honest conversations with. Discomfort, or the avoidance of it, often pairs with defensiveness.

She looks out the window at our waitress who is with another table before saying more. *"I can't remember a time when I didn't feel ashamed for being too Brown. Even when I'm trying to look and act as white as possible, the expectations around my body, speech, grades, career—hell, literally everything—were all there simply so I could become more palatable for white people. Any success I had was seen as a derivative from being part of white culture."*

Her next sentence imprints on my memory. As soon as she says it I have the distinct body response of knowing I'll never forget her voice and words: *"On a very big and deep level, whiteness has denied me knowing who I am. The expectation to conform has cost me my language, culture and truest identity."*

She went on to describe boundary violations and entitlement she encounters at work, school and church—essentially everywhere public. One specific experience she shares involves months of microaggressions she and another woman of culture experienced at work. V decided to address it with the white women who ran the business. Not only did they deflect responsibility for the ways they were maintaining an unsafe space they proceeded to gaslight V for her experience. When she held her ground one white woman finally resorted to tears, *"How else are white people supposed to do better if they're going to be criticized for doing it wrong and no one will teach them?"*

I feel sick to my stomach as she continues sharing, infuriated on her behalf. The sensations my body is experiencing carries the familiarity I now recognize as an invitation. I sit with the question—where and how do I dismiss feedback when it's offered me about *me*? I have to assume I have parts of myself that would rather avoid accountability, seasons in my life, past or present, where I've neglected or half-assed investigating the ways I've participated in harm regardless of my intentions. In fact it's fair to assume there are still closets full

A House Of Mirrors

of fragility inside my body I've maladaptively learned to bypass as a way of maintaining comfort rather than reckoning with my power and insecurities.

V's words continued replaying in my head long after our breakfast ended: *"whiteness has denied me knowing who I am"*. The reality is that supremacy in all its forms denies people their true identity and full humanity.

In order to dehumanize others and center whiteness, people in power must abandon their humanity too, mirroring the impact of patriarchy: no one actually wins. *We are all a lesser version of ourselves when disconnected from our bodies and humanity*—unable to see and value others' bodies and full humanity as a result. If we don't know how to settle our discomfort and mature our fragility we cannot tell ourselves the truth of our stories, history or hear the truth of others' experiences with racism and prejudice. If we don't become more embodied we cannot connect to our inner *'yes, no and maybe'* nor honor another's practice with consent and boundaries. Our world and culture remain compromised, we are all harmed—yet not all harmed equally.

I finish up my last week of interviews during a warm week in May when the desert jumps radically from spring to summer. Circumstances dictate doing the interviews virtually from my husband's home office, the walls of which are deep blue and display a number of records and guitars. Most participants start the conversation more interested in the instruments than my questions. Today, with only a few remaining interviews left, I discover I'm still not even a teeny bit weary of asking these same twelve questions. Each participants' responses have offered insight and been an invitation to stay open, curious and more importantly, humble.

About a third of the way through the conversation, Marcus begins describing the heightened awareness he feels when he's romantically been involved with a white woman. He never wants to cause harm, however when he dates white women he feels even more aware of what's at stake if the person he's dating were to feel hurt or rejected—the potential impact of what a false accusation about his character or behavior could do to him hangs present, loaded.

The history of white women falsely accusing Black men of violence in the United States is many centuries old and as a forty-seven year old Black man,

Mel Gentry Bosna

Marcus regularly navigates the risks involved with occupying a body white people misinterpret as a threat.

Rather than imagine though, I shift my body in the office chair and ask him instead, "if you're willing and feel comfortable enough to share more, tell me how living with that tension impacts you."

He takes a deep breath, breaking eye contact momentarily before responding, *"I'm a person concerned with others' comfort. I want people to feel good, safe, have a good time—if I felt like a woman wasn't into what we were doing I wouldn't push it, and while I think it's because I'm a stand-up guy, I can also see that for me it's tied to being Black."*

As he's speaking I tune into my body, practice awareness of my whiteness, notice the energy I feel in this conversation, the places I feel uncomfortable. I hold these parts next to the weight of his lived reality and drop deeper into my breathe with the intention of staying open and soft. "Say more if it feels right."

He slowly nods his head, hands rest across his chest. *"I understand there's a shorter leash for me in society than others. An assumption about me or a misstep could literally end my life. There's no room for Black men to mess up, all it takes is one phone call you know, one call and it's over, my life could be over."*

He went on to share ways white supremacy regularly impacts his stress level, influencing how he interacts with others, makes it difficult to practice trust and vulnerability. It's hard to let one's guard down when hypervigilant, hard to settle an activated nervous system when the threat is not simply anticipated but in actuality, very real. The bodies of Black and Indigenous people are at higher risk of being harmed and both the history and continued reality lives inside bodies of culture. The violence that white supremacy perpetuates lives inside white bodies too.

Anti-Blackness is embedded in United States' history, policies and institutions and therefore exists inside us all. The ways white women weaponize their tears and contribute to need to be named. Crimes motivated by misogyny, ableism, homophobia, sexism, etc. are all valid in scope *and* impact. However, this section aims to name how consent and boundaries may be harder to access and express for bodies of culture as a direct result of racialized violence.

A House Of Mirrors

I've listened as clients, research participants and dear friends alike have shared experiences with being targeted, harassed, assaulted, and later gaslighted by white bodied people, some of whom were strangers, most however who were people with whom they were or are in personal relationship with. I believe them—which is important and also *not* enough.

It's critical for those of us in white presenting bodies to own, reckon and decolonize the ways we participate, perpetuate and benefit from white supremacy. It's an invitation and a responsibility to call ourselves and communities into reparative accountability—we must understand the ways in which *all* systems of racial supremacy in general and white supremacy very specifically hijack reciprocal practices of consent.

The need is for white people to lean-in and do the internal, relational and communal work, own the ways white supremacy is threaded inside their bodies and stories, and deepen into greater presence and belonging with others. As we become more embodied we become less willing to bypass the ways we hold and abuse power and can *only* *then* start to become safer for others. This is how we create a sense of collective belonging which stops us from terrorizing others.

In his book *The Quaking of America*, Resmaa Manakem writes:

> *There's a way out of this mess, and it requires each of us to begin with our own body. You and your body are important parts of the solution. You will not just read this book; you will experience it in your body. Your body–all of our bodies–are where changing the status quo must begin.*

As previously mentioned I've been deeply influenced by Resmaa's work and include this specific quote because it highlights how, while intellectualized anti-racism work is important, it will not dismantle white supremacy unless we integrate it into an embodied practice within places it most resides, namely white bodies. For example, many police officers may not consciously identify or see themselves as racist yet may react to embedded fear and internalized prejudicial beliefs nonetheless. Beliefs alone, like bodies, are neither the problem nor the solution. Learning how to become embodied while assuming there are places of vulnerability, fear, shame and insecurity within us that have and will continue to cause harm *actually* makes us safer. Denying that these parts exist within us means we have power we've neither reckoned with nor stewarded well, which inevitably surfaces as a weapon when threatened.

My hope is that this chapter was disruptive for all of us but white women especially—we can become more embodied, integrity is worth the disruption of owning the ways we participate in harm. *Actual* safety for those who live in bodies of culture ought to be the priority. I believe we can and must develop the skills to unwaveringly examine our reflection when it's shown to us.

May we all become unflinching containers worthy of bearing our weight, holding the truth and in the process, discover that when we belong more deeply to ourselves we no longer need to belong to any other power outside us, white supremacy included. We can handle knowing the truth about ourselves, our history and our present reality because we refuse to abandon our *truest* selves.

When we do this work we will be the first in any room to confess our own name, shed old unfitting skin, hold our feet compassionately yet relentlessly to the fire. We learn to agitate and protest against every system that would ask us to reduce our and others' wholeness. I am imperfectly, awkwardly leaning into this yet committed nonetheless—join me.

Part III: A House Restored

"be easy.
take your time.
you are coming
home
to yourself."

—Nayyirah Waheed

Chapter Six

REPARATIVE ACCOUNTABILITY

"You don't have to worry about burning bridges, if you're building your own"

—Kerry E. Wagner

NOTHING DROWNS THE OCEAN

The overwhelm that occurs when we realize consent has been violated and a boundary has been trespassed may hijack us from staying within our bodies, triggering a trauma response. This overwhelm happens when we've been the one violated and it can also occur when we recognize *we ourselves have done the violating*, intentional or not. Overwhelm is often the body's protective response, yet may also prevent us from moving through our emotions to a place where we can care for the injury, whether ours or others. This chapter is for those of us in search of a path back from harm but who are seemingly stuck within the overwhelm and uncertainty of it all.

I see this daily in my office. Overwhelm and dissociation are perhaps the most visible symptoms of trauma I witness. Other common symptoms may include pervasive guilt, shame, intrusive thoughts, nightmares, flashbacks, blame, depersonalization, minimization and outright denial. In fact, as a direct response to things our body experiences as traumatic, our brain may store memory in such a way we seemingly even forget what happened—not because the experience has been healed or we weren't significantly impacted but rather due to a part of us that fears we cannot handle what happened or the feelings that coincide with it.

Our brains may therefore tuck experiences away from our memory while storing them in our bodies nonetheless. This isn't faulty, this is the wisdom of our best interpretation in any given moment, it's an adaptive way humans survive until we can more fully recover. A loose definition of trauma I use with clients is that trauma is that which the body interprets, experiences and stores as threatening rather than releasing and resetting to safety.

I started using a metaphor awhile back that for the life of me I can't remember if I came up with solely on my own, was handed by another clinician or borrowed somewhere from mythology—the metaphor has certainly evolved in form and detail over use and I've loved seeing how each person it's shared with adapts it to reflect a personal narrative of their story. I used it last year during a session when Jade came into the office.

I could tell something was off within seconds after she walked in and sat down, an emotion was surfacing that appeared very tender—she'd been doing steady, beautiful reclamation work the last two years, now when she's blended with her powerlessness it's quickly visible as it no longer appears familiar to her personality or energy.

"What's wrong?" I ask gently, wanting her to feel I'm tuned in. My heart feels steady, ready to support whatever she's willing to share. Jade curls up under a tasseled blanket, stares sweetly yet sadly at our office therapy puppy, and whispers "*We have to put the dog down.*" Tears immediately follow.

Anyone who loves a pet knows the significance of this layered loss. I know Jade's story well enough to understand the layers of trauma, attachment, displaced guilt and dormant grief are tangled up in her relationship with her dogs. This impending loss is loaded with more than one storyline and wave of pain, many of my clients relate to it. Within seconds she's moved from crying to what's appearing as an anxiety attack, the emotions rolling in bigger and more intense as she begins to anticipate having to survive another heartache.

We use grounding skills to come back to the room and more importantly, her body, breathing and co-regulating together. I only then offer her the metaphor that's often helped me. The hope is that it will reduce the overwhelm of her anticipatory grief, however we start with something that historically has been vulnerable but is not currently an active issue in her life as a way of staying grounded.

"Jade, will you experiment with me for a bit? We'll come back to your grief eventually when you're ready to but I'd like to explore something else first. Let's say every feeling and wound is somehow represented by something that exists in the ocean. For instance, if you were to describe your anxiety about getting on an airplane, what thing in the ocean could represent that specific anxiety?"

She pauses, stares at the window, laughs a little and says *"Well it used to be something HORRIBLE, like a scaley eel but now it's more like a snappy little crab!"* We laugh and I guide us on. "What about the eating disorder part of you, what might represent that?"

Again, she pauses, reflecting before she responds, *"It still feels like a shark that's circling, waiting to see if I'm actually strong enough and committed to letting myself feel comfortable and safe in my body—almost as if it wants to know if I'm a match for the way it wants to protect me."*

From here we continue exploring and Jade leans into the storytelling nature of the metaphor, naming different layers of past trauma as different things. One part of her past feels like a darkness weighted on the ocean floor, something she can't necessarily see but feels akin to a sunken ship still unsafe to explore. She describes her history of panic attacks like a strong currant that literally takes her away from where she wants to be, schools of fish that are playful but that seem lost in the expanse of all the other big predators that intrude.

I make sure it's clear that we're not going to process any memories associated with the things we're naming, we're assigning each part their role in the metaphor, witnessing their existence without diving any deeper into the emotions and sensations they hold. When I ask about the part of her that feels guilty, responsible for bad things that've happened in her life she looks at me, eyes pooling with tears, and describes it as *"the seaweed I can't untangle myself from, no matter how hard I seem to try."*

Lastly, together we name the overwhelm of it all—the current, anticipatory grief of this season that exists alongside the layers of past trauma. The overwhelm feels like the movement a whale creates when approaching—gigantic, massive, threatening in scope. Even if she *knows* whales aren't predatory, even if she understands the whale doesn't intend her harm, it doesn't initially matter because she feels the whale is still sure to drown her anyways due to its size.

"Jade?" She looks at me, her body sad but now more settled.

"Where do you identify yourself in this metaphor?"

Her eyes widen, surprised as though it had been a given. She shrugs her shoulders, says *"I guess I don't know…something…small?"*

Shaking my head gently, intentionally, I smile and say "Nope. I don't think so, in fact I think that may be part of why this all feels so overwhelming."

I continue, "I don't see you as a small fish, nor as a diver lost at sea. You are not weak and powerless trapped by seaweed, nor are you held hostage in that sunken ship—parts of you *feel* this, I get you and understand why. You're not crazy nor lost—the reason this all feels SO overwhelming is because in your intention to survive you've lost touch with who you are—you're disconnected from the *powerful source* of yourself that's always existed inside you. You are not something that can be threatened by anything in the waters you named, because you Jade are the furthest thing from small and easily devoured—you are, in fact the *WHOLE. GODDAMN. OCEAN.*"

She's crying at this point but her tears now reflect a different emotion, my voice is heavier too as I'm also emotional. I deeply want her to hear how I see and know her, that I mean every bit. I continue, "Nothing can sink the ocean, nothing can drown the ocean! *NOTHING.* You are big, expansive, deep and wide, you are *already* the container of everything you hold. Things will surface, sometimes pass through on a current, outright disrupt your waters—but literally nothing can drown nor destroy you, you are so much bigger than what's happened to you and everything you contain. There is no wave you cannot outride, no storm that

121

won't eventually settle, no depth of yourself off limits from exploring—and—you never, *ever* have to feel it all at once or before you discern you're ready to. I'm simply here, reminding you that if and when you choose to witness what's inside you, it will have less power and feel less disrupted when you remember who you are. It doesn't have the power to drown you—you are the ocean."

OUR BODY'S RESPONSE

We cannot begin to face the harm done to us nor own and repair harm we've done to others without a clearer sense of ourselves *outside* of our trauma and the moral injuries we participate in. Without clarity about our value and core identity we will inevitably feel like we're drowning in shame and overwhelm and subsequently feel like we have to check-out, deny or dissociate from the emotion. We will interpret others who are offering feedback to us as a threat, as though they too are trying to drown us. I've felt like I'd drown before if I felt how sad I actually was—I've also been perceived by others as out to drown them when I've called them into the work of accountability.

When something bad happens many of us disconnect from it, exiling it away. But when we do this we won't be able to retrieve these parts of ourselves without a clear sense that we're worth rescuing and redeeming. Trauma violates our consent and the social and relational contracts we have with others, which diminishes hope that we can have, deserve and choose better outcomes moving forward.

I have both experienced and observed others avoid their personal healing as well as neglect repair with others because of overwhelm and disconnect from self. I have deep compassion for why we humans do this, believing most people want relief yet don't know how to approach it without becoming flooded by their emotions.

Mel Gentry Bosna

Herein lies the danger with continuing this pattern: what we cannot face, we cannot repair—which inevitably defines the limits we can access consent and practice it with others.

Meaning, what we've denied or deflected can't be healed, what we refuse to recognize as harmed we can't reclaim, what we dismiss won't be restored to safety. When we remain compartmentalized and disembodied we don't have access to our whole self and therefore can't practice full-bodied, reciprocal consent. The degree of honesty our *'yes, no and maybe'* holds exists in *direct* proportion with our ability to be with ourselves, including both the parts that experienced harmed and participated in harmed. We cannot ever do this all at once yet the invitation to engage in embodied, reparative accountability is the way forward if we want to reduce harm in the world. This is the path offered to reset ourselves and our communities back to safety.

A third-way approach is an alternative to the traditional binary options offered, which I first learned about from Rob Bell's teachings years ago. Third-way means that rather than see our options dualisticly, either right *or* wrong, good *or* bad, all *or* nothing, we can instead engage in broad curiosity surrounding what alternative practices might present themselves. It invites dialectical thinking and emboldens creativity while centering harm reduction. Much of what we've been taught collectively about repair derives from a binary framework—either the person who caused the harm is "canceled" for their wrong-doing or, is prematurely reinstated back to a position of power after a rushed apology. Neither resets anyone to safety which is what I define the goal to be with reparative accountability and consent practices.

I'd like to differentiate my use of 'cancel culture' from mainstream critiques of the terms. I've seen it dismissed as a made up phenomenon lacking real weight and consequence. Alternatively, I've heard it defined as censorship with the power to destroy reputations instantaneously. These definitions lack curiosity regarding the ways we're collectively trying to hold each other accountable and the complexities surrounding where we're stuck.

Cancel culture in itself is a trauma response as is welcoming someone back to a relationship or position of power prematurely when they've yet to do any work *outside of* apologizing. In fact, there are five common trauma responses humans experience when harm is caused, all of which are the body's best effort to help

123

us navigate something that feels threatening and disruptive to us—cancel culture folds within and overlaps these five responses.

These responses are evolutionary, biological and adaptive. None of them are bad or superior to each other—when we experience a trauma response, we can generously assume that in that given moment our bodies assessed and reacted on our behalf as safely as it felt possible. We are all genuinely doing the best we can, therefore the goal isn't to 'do better', it's to become safer.

Below is a brief summary of five common trauma and stress responses. It bears repeating, none of them are cognitive responses the thinking parts of our brain choose but adaptive responses driven by the discernment of our bodies:

> *FIGHT*: In situations where we feel we have the ability to fight back successfully and/or overpower the threat our body may mobilize into action.

> *FLIGHT:* In situations we may flee where we don't feel equipped to fight or find it necessary, getting farther away from what feels like a threat in order to achieve safety.

> *FREEZE:* In situations we feel we can neither successfully fight back nor run away from our body responds by preserving all its energy resources and freezing. Many of us dissociate in this trauma response as a proactive way to feel less harm.

> *FLOCK:* Most of us have witnessed babies and young children do this! When something threatening or disarming happens the natural inclination is to look or reach towards safe people for reassurance that we're okay. We do this as humans throughout our life span, looking for both

reassurance we're safe as well as validation that something threatening is happening.

FAWN: This response occurs when the safest option is to try and deescalate the threat–often done through ego stroking, agreeing, soothing or reassuring the person threatening us as a means to try and either get away once they're calm and/or have the violation be less violent. This can look like people-pleasing, placating or even flirting when there's no way to escape the threatening situation.

Many of my clients come to therapy berating themselves for how they've responded when something scary or threatening happened. I see evidence of it often enough in my own life too.

Years ago while at the gym I found myself feeling trapped on a stair climbing machine next to a group of men near the racquetball courts. Every Sunday from what I observed, this group of men in their 60s-70s gathered and played in teams with each other. The stair climber available to me that day happened to be closest to where they were standing which is how I found myself in such close proximity.

At one point they were passing around one of the men's phone and it became clear they were viewing pornography together. The group laughed, commenting on what they were watching, in turn I looked around to see if anyone else was aware of their behavior (Flock response). When I saw that no one else was paying attention my body froze—not in a complete and absolute sense, thankfully I didn't tumble off the machine. Nonetheless I froze up internally. I did not want to be in such close proximity to a group of older men making demeaning comments towards women's bodies and yet couldn't seem to get myself off that damn machine and away from them.

I just…*stayed*, kept on climbing, acutely aware of their raucous laughter and the edginess of their energy. My muscles were tense, my movement was repetitive until eventually the group moved on and I moved away.

Later on I found my partner who was working out in another area of the gym and shared what had happened. He couldn't *believe* that 'the feisty, feminist, women's advocate, enneagram 8' he experiences me as didn't just give that group of old men a piece of her mind. To be fair, I was also struggling to process why I hadn't done or said anything either and had started to cycle into a shame spiral about it. Why *had* I stayed?

Texting with my friend Venessa later that day clarified what was happening in my body–in a split second when it appeared no one else was either aware or going to intervene with this inappropriate scene my body decided, on my behalf, that the seemingly safest option was to preserve my resources and be as invisible and small as possible in order to make my way through that situation. (Freeze response

In contrast, two weeks later at the same gym I was using a particular weight machine when an older white man walked over to me and aggressively tried to rush along my workout despite the fact I'd only completed two out of the three sets I'd set out to do. He acted entitled towards the machine and my personal space however that time my body accessed a different response than previously with the racquetball crew, seemingly feeling less threatened—I went on to respectfully let that motherfucker know he could damn well wait until I was done with the machine. (Fight response

Similar situations, same physical environment, yet different responses based on my body's discernment on what was safest for me–I have gratitude and compassion for myself now when considering both of the ways my body showed up on my behalf to try and keep me safe. Perhaps on another day leaving the space (Flight or placating the man (Fawn would've presented like good options, I can't say since after that second incident I stopped going to that gym.

THIRD-WAY: REJECTING THE BINARY

Let's come back to what's vulnerable about cancel culture. I get the urge and action to cancel someone, it feels *righteous*–removing someone from having access to yourself or others can feel like the most liberating and just way to respond and, at times, extreme and absolute boundaries *are* appropriate. At its core cancel culture is rooted in a desire to ensure our safety and so rigid boundaries are erected to keep said person out–with it though often comes a label of the exiled person as *BAD* and if we're not careful, a practice of dehumanization towards the 'bad person' follows in order to ensure they stay over *there,* far away so they don't ever hurt us again.

Boundaries at their core are the outward expression of consent. If consent is our internal '*yes, no and maybe*' then boundaries are our external expression of the internal process, they allow us to honor ourselves and others and are meant to be a way to *stay* in a relationship as opposed to having to leave it.

A boundary is needed in cases where trust is eroded and we've been harmed— canceling someone's humanity however is not a boundary as much as it at times may *feel* like the way to set one. Boundaries are meant to protect our time, energy, property and body, they are meant to be clear and help us thrive in community.

A permanent boundary may be absolutely essential with someone who harmed us–you'll never find me arguing to allow someone to have access to you that you don't feel safe around. Oftentimes though we ostracize people out of a place of fear and rage rather than from a deep and clear source of wisdom. The expression of the boundary may initially appear the same on the surface in both instances, however the underbelly holds an entirely different energy and it's important we know how to examine it otherwise we'll get stuck in it.

The problem with cancel culture is that in our woundedness we respond by using boundaries as weapons instead of delineations–we cancel not just the behavior but people themselves, sending them away. Dependent on whether that person does their work to own and hold themselves accountable or regards themself somehow as a victim of having been canceled may determine whether they continue to perpetuate the same cycle of behaviors in a new community. How many times have we seen this happen? Too many to count.

Alternatively, I've watched communities and corporations alike align with a person causing harm right after receiving a baseline apology–this is rooted more or less in Freeze, Fawn and/or Flock trauma responses. If we are attached to the person or the power the person holds, then we are more likely to disconnect from our own needs for safety and instead remain attached to their presence even if it compromises our own wellness and values. We may placate, dismiss, minimize or outright deny the harm caused on the premise that they're a *GOOD* person instead of a *BAD* person and therefore their behavior somehow becomes less problematic since we've shifted the conversation away from what caused harm and instead are debating someone's humanity and identity.

What I propose is an alternative way, a third-way that neither swings hard left nor right but finds the messy middle of liminal space. I've wrestled with this concept intentionally over the last several years in my personal relationships, trying to hold space for this middle ground that feels holy and uncharted since we haven't seen it modeled often enough. What does it mean to call someone into their integrity as opposed to simply pushing them away instead?

In 2021 I witnessed reparative accountability in practice after receiving a message from a friend about a musical artist whose work had been meaningful to our deconstruction process from fundamentalism. Her message read, "someone is accusing him of rape and I believe her." Within minutes of listening to Kelly's live video I believed her too. It's not my job to investigate, prove, try or sentence anyone–that is essentially what cancel culture would have us practice.

It is however my responsibility to pay attention, stay in my own body, listen to my intuition and discern outcomes and boundaries in alignment with what I sense and know—to this day I haven't seen a survivor stay as authentically embodied as Kelly did while talking about an assault she'd experienced, which is one reason her story imprinted strongly and so immediately for me. I don't have to determine his intent because I believe her when she describes the impact.

I am neither the expert nor the judge of anyone's life. I felt intuitively that Kelly was present in her body and clear emotionally. She appears to have done the tender, hard and intentional work of being present with her trauma which eventually empowered her to recover from it. One of the remarkable things she communicated was an invitation for both her abuser and his community to lean in and do better. At no point did she come off as being out for blood or to ruin his reputation—hell, she didn't even seem invested in justice given how unclear and unsatisfying justice is in situations of sexual violence.

Kelly clearly, respectfully and relentlessly shared her experience and then surrendered it to tens of thousands of witnesses. Unanchored to the outcome, she had already chosen her healing separate from his response. She wasn't out to destroy him nor his career, rather she called him to the table and the broader community into the fold of third-way accountability. Kelly appeared invested in collective reckoning—what would we do and who did we want to become now that we knew about this harm?

She wrote in the video caption words I still reflect on today: "*Ejecting people from community doesn't heal the collective. Sweeping it under the rug doesn't either.*" The liminal space of third-way accountability is messier since we're shifting from a binary, black and white, all-or-nothing framework and exploring instead how to see each other's full humanity while telling the truth about our humanity and experience.

I related deeply, reflecting on an email I had sent my family when I began unraveling my own childhood trauma. I wrote my intention to heal regardless if they supported or believed my story as experienced from my *body's* perspective. We can't heal relationships or culture without others' ownership and participation, however we can and must heal ourselves regardless if others do their part. This is possible when we anchor our healing to our own power, care and self-validation.

I wrote the following words in an email, "I intend to heal with or without you" from what seemed the same energy Kelly embodied in her Instagram video. I now understand and identify this energy as self-accountability in its purest expression. Holding ourselves to the wake, quake and goddamn reckoning of our own healing no matter who joins in nor what disruption befalls us. We can see, integrate and own it as the path forward—hoping others join but decidedly committed either way.

Kelly and I both understand consent and boundary violations are often served up in ways mainstream culture minimizes and invalidates. The reality being that all our bodies know when something unsafe and threatening is happening to us and, if more of us were *actually* present in our bodies, had the skills to navigate our emotions and were awake to the power dynamics existing among us, we'd also better discern what was happening inside the bodies of those around us. I believe the man who harmed Kelly had parts of him that knew better, parts of him that may not have fully understood consent due to his own religious upbringing and parts that also appeared to not *want to know* based on the minimizing response he offered when exposed.

A House Restored

We don't get to determine what a good enough response is for others, especially those who have been directly harmed—I can tell you what I would've liked to have heard from him instead of the denial he offered. Had he responded by saying "*I am deeply grieved by the harm I've caused Kelly—directly with my behavior and indirectly through my avoidance of accountability. I am committed to holding this pain now while also working through my shame. Women deserve to feel and be safe in this world and specifically in their interactions with me. I'm willing to do what I was too ashamed to do before, which is to hear how others have experienced me and work on the issues inside me that caused harm.*"

Kelly later volunteered to participate in the research project and all that's included here is shared with her consent. You may ask what permission he's given—which initially appears a fair enough question. While everyone has a right to name themselves and share their side of a story, I do not adhere to all experiences deserving equitable airtime or space. I've said it throughout and will say it again, intention matters, *impact matters more.*

Intentions are more often than not complex and nuanced. If we're not careful we fixate on intentions to determine the validity and extent of the harm caused which all parties involved are vulnerable to do–the person harmed, the person who caused the harm and the bystander witnesses which serve as judge and jury. Over-emphasizing intentions however is *not* the same experience and conversation our bodies are having inside us, which is why intellectually understanding things will never bring repair or reset our bodies to safety–trauma is stored in the body and focusing on intentions collectively robs us of repair.

Owning our stories makes us safer, wiser people–instead of presuming somehow we can avoid ever causing harm we are better off assuming that we unintentionally and regretfully will cause harm. We can then proactively develop skills that aid in building shame resilience, integrity, humility and self-accountability.

When I hear a man presume misogyny and patriarchy exist within him and watch him hold himself accountable before anyone else has to, I see him as safe and trustworthy. Similarly, when I witness white people presume racism and prejudice live inside their bodies and watch them regularly go in looking for it, seemingly unsurprised when it surfaces I discern opportunities to build trust. When people are offered feedback and respond with humility and curiosity, my body feels settled in ways that allows me to more easily access my needs and boundaries. Our communities are safer, richer and freer when we can explore our internal worlds and take responsibility for our external behaviors. We all win.

While the man who harmed Kelly is entitled to his own version of events, the experience of the person with more power who more directly caused harm will *never* be equitable to the person who received harmed. This will never be a '*he said/she said*' situation given the grossly disproportionate impact to those involved, existing power dynamics, and the *statistical data* regarding the rarity of false accusations made in cases of sexual assault. I don't need to hear his perspective to believe her.

I had been a fan of his music for several years. When I explored my body's responses to the information Kelly disclosed I felt sad, nauseated and dissatisfied with the options presented with holding him responsible. Unless he is going to hold *himself* to a higher standard of integrity and the people he's in direct relationship with call him into deeper healing work nothing actually changes.

Even still, I could not continue listening to his music and remain in alignment. Unless there was evidence of proactive self-accountability backed by evidence from the women harmed that he was making repairs then I would be listening to music I enjoyed but doing so *outside* of my own values. In other words, it would diminish me to do so, I'd have to make myself smaller and disembodied.

While I can't directly hold him accountable to any actionable step, I can hold *myself* accountable by choosing to stay in alignment with my integrity, refusing to participate in anything *less* than what feels safe, clear and full of character. Our bodies will tell us if and when we're doing this which is why embodiment practices are so crucial—we practice consent from our deepest selves by increasing our ability and capacity to be with ourselves.

I hear and observe people diminish this step all the time, "*what good will come of it, I'm only one person*". People abandon the work when it feels 'too big, too vague or too personal.' Often it's expressed with broader social issues related to politics, consumerism or work culture–it plays out in community, social and family dynamics though too. "*What good is it to push back when so many others still support and enable that ideology, what good is it if I already know that person isn't going to change.*"

This defeatism is a reflection of displaced power, feeling that in order for change or healing to happen others have to do their part first. While this is true of collective healing, we can practice holding ourselves accountable to what's good, right, pure and true. When we refuse to participate in harm on personal levels more safety is still achieved.

Later that year I had the opportunity to reckon with my own lines around accountability and question how I wanted to lean into them. I found myself in a unique situation within my community—people whom I had completely separate relationships with experienced harm in a relationship they were in with each other. Due to being in relationship with all parties I was afforded not only the opportunity to engage with each of them but also the delineated responsibility of exploring and calling in the power differentials as I saw them.

I wrestled for months with what my role was—it felt clear to me that boundaries and consent had not been honored, however I wasn't present when the violation happened, wasn't a person directly involved, how could I from the outside of things assess and discern what'd actually been experienced? I kept reflecting on what part, if any, actually belonged to me, and where and how to stay in my lane.

It would've honestly been simpler, easier to bow out and not get involved in an effort to try and preserve my separate relationship with each of them. However when present with my emotions and body, I knew instinctively that opting out would be participating in harm. I loved and valued each person involved, it was *because* of this deep affection that I chose to trust my intuition and practice an embodied consent by calling my friends into ongoing, disruptive conversations. The goal was for everyone to experience safety and thrive in our community.

I wasn't out for blood or to slap anyone's wrist. While parts of me wanted to bypass involvement, my integrity would not, *could not,* loosen her grip. Reparative accountability aims to shift the energy. The work doesn't involve ultimatums, metaphorically tying a noose around anyone's neck—the grip I felt had more to do with the hold I had on my own character. I wrestled with the following questions: On whose behalf am I disrupting things? On whose behalf am I remaining silent? Who do I want to be and how can I practice alignment? It became increasingly clear for me that choosing silence would be a way of bypassing work that actually belonged to *ME,* and in so doing, also enable others I loved to bypass work that belonged to them as well.

I spent eight months wrestling with this—processed things with my own therapist, fleshed it out with a few trusted confidants, continued to peel back the layers of my beliefs around accountability and hoped-longed-risked for the best possible outcome as I could discern. Eventually the conversations devolved and it became clear that the invitation before me was with letting go: we cannot hold others accountable if they are neither willing nor ready to hold themselves accountable. Continuing to try results in forcing change and violating a relationship's consent and boundaries. What I can do is hold myself accountable with delineating the lines of relationship and consent I am willing to participate in.

This means extending invitation for relationships within the lines of reciprocal consent—simultaneously accepting that if someone isn't ready, willing or able to respond to what's being offered I must grieve and release them, the growth is not mine to steward. Harm unfortunately is inevitable, we all cause it despite our best efforts not to. We're better off accepting and having compassion for ourselves and others *while* developing an internal structure of shame resilience that can tolerate the emotions we encounter when harm happens.

Moving through those tender, hard conversations allowed my needs around repair and accountability to take more clarifying shape. I don't get to determine what someone else needs in order for a relationship to feel safe enough to return to, it's personal and unique to each person's story—to presume a formula for others' needs or what's 'good enough' is its own form of gaslighting.

When done from a place of embodiment I believe it begins with the following: the person who caused harm takes a long, hard PAUSE after receiving feedback. No defense—no rushed apology—no discussion of intentions. They lean into the space a pause offers the body and begin to sit and sift what comes up before reacting, defending or explaining themselves.

On a social level we often see people who, when called to account, react prematurely with an apology motivated by their fear with being 'canceled,' criticized, ostracized, left behind and pushed out. When this happens there is a rush to apologize before enough time has been spent with ourselves. This pause creates the space and opportunity to sit and wade through what was happening within us that caused harm and in turn led to a betrayal of our own values and subsequently led us to trespass on another's boundaries. This is often a reactionary and involuntary stress and trauma response to avoid threat, other times it may also be a result of parts of us that are intolerant of feeling vulnerability or shame so we deflect, avoid and minimize the impact of the harm caused.

Does that mean when offered feedback or called into accountability people should stay silent and disappear? Of course not! An initial response is needed *as soon* as it's accessible to offer one from a place that isn't dismissive nor defensive.

This might sound something along these lines: *"I hate that I hurt you, thank you for sharing. I am willing to listen and may also take a step back to explore what was going on inside me when I caused you harm so I don't keep doing it. I don't want to offer a rushed or incomplete apology because you deserve better than that—is there anything you need from me right now to feel safer and know I'm taking this seriously?"*

After someone has taken time and effort to pause, reflect and consider what was happening inside their body when they caused another person harm, they can then and only then cycle back and ask, *"I've had some time to reflect and get some feedback from other people invested in my integrity. I'm willing to listen if you have more to share. You don't owe me your time and energy. I now understand what was happening inside me and why I violated your consent and boundaries. Would it be helpful to hear what I learned about myself and how I caused harm or is that something I need to keep to myself—I can see how it could come off as a justification and want to defer to whatever feels like it best honors you."*

The person harmed may or may not be willing to engage in repair depending on the harm caused and how safe and supported they feel with reentering proximity and relationships. The community's job is less about investigating the transgressions and more aptly to prioritize, protect and safeguard those vulnerable. No one ought to determine what others need in order to feel that safety has been reestablished—the person who caused harm may feel frustrated about the timeline, overwhelmed by the requests and needs expressed from others and perhaps feel shamed by bystanders for how they're navigating accountability however within a consent framework it's imperative that we center and respond from deep empathy and deference to those with seemingly the least amount of safety and power.

The hope of reparative accountability is for everyone to return to a deeper sense of safety internally, and when possible, to return to an experience of safety relationally and within the community. This isn't always possible due to how power dynamics play out, who power elects to protect and the ways western culture avoids vulnerability due to shame and fear.

No one owes us a relationship.

We owe no one a relationship.

NO ONE.

We do, however, *owe each other safety.*

It bears repeating since we often think an apology or even full accountability resets us to safety. We must hold with deep regard the central understanding that having access to others is not our right–it's a privilege, a gift and one we approach with the respect and dignity humans deserve. Giving others access to ourselves is not a cheap exchange nor is access to ourselves an irrevocable action to be taken for granted. The person harmed is the sole determiner regarding whether they are willing to re-engage in a relationship.

Even when forgiveness and compassion are accessible and offered we *still do not owe* people relationships or proximity to our bodies, even when people are sad, genuinely sorry, they are still not owed proximity or relationship with our children. Sorrow and guilt are not healthy benchmarks for reentry–ownership, self-accountability and an acceptance of and follow-through with boundaries are clearer indicators of safety and our bodies tell us if we feel in alignment with moving forward if we are wise enough to listen to them.

Access is earned through humility, trust and consistent acts of safety that mirror consent and honor boundaries over time and even then we may determine it's beyond our willingness and effort to explore. If a person who caused harm genuinely feels like they've done their work to repair things and feels like what they are being asked to do and give is more than what feels safe and in alignment for them then they too can reevaluate the dynamics and choose to not reengage. No one owes another person a relationship, especially when to offer one would compromise safety, integrity, dignity and humanity.

A House Restored

Should we decide to reenter a relationship after harm has been caused? We ought to look for the type of ownership I previously highlighted–I want to hear someone say with a *mouthful* of clarity and accountability what they did that contributed to harm, what was going on inside them before, during, and after they caused harm and what their plan is for reducing the vulnerabilities surrounding it moving forward. If a person can access a sense of internal security, they will remain open to ongoing feedback about what feels safe or concerning within the relationship.

Even when repair happens and we choose to reenter relationships and community, the opportunities to reflect, reevaluate and delineate needs around consent and boundaries continue. Nothing is absolute, fixed, permanent or guaranteed ongoing status.

I've grieved and let go of relationships I previously thought were safer than they turned out to actually be when tested. I have had to set boundaries, walk away and accept the reality of others' limits, often including my own. I've also experienced sweet surprises along the way when people I didn't anticipate being open or willing to do the work ended up engaging in self-accountability and it deepened our relationship as a result.

Oftentimes I think we're given an idea that once we've 'healed' a wound, we won't have big emotions or reactions however that's not necessarily the case. I spent a weekend last year visiting my parents in the rural mountain town they now live in. While there I found myself feeling wave after wave of grief as I confronted new realizations about things I hadn't previously been able or willing to see–the difference was that previously such feelings or memories would've triggered a trauma response and I would've likely been reactive towards my parents, edgy and unkind.

However, this trip felt different. I found myself tenderly feeling deep sadness, however I also discovered my heart to be so…soft. Not once did I feel my body react or "light up" from a triggered place–some of that is because of the ways in which I've learned to call my parents into their work and mirror back the places I've felt harmed. Much of that however was due to my own healing work of being able to be in my own body and care for my own needs and pain. Determining what my inner '*yes, no and maybe*' sounds like has empowered me to advocate on my behalf and in turn draw boundaries more kindly and graciously as needed. This healing has come directly from holding myself accountable to my own healing work.

Learning how to safely be with my emotions and body's sensations, discerning my inner voice, recognizing needs, increasing curiosity and practicing compassion about the places I trespass my own consent alongside others' boundaries has allowed me a deeper ability to self-govern. This internal sovereignty has in turn allowed me to enter into relationships with others in a way where I feel more grounded and experience fewer trauma responses due to overall feeling less triggered.

I know who I am and therefore own more accurately the harm I cause others in ways that, hopefully, make me a safer person for others to be around and in relationship with. I will never be immune or exempt from causing harm nor will you. We can and must become a people willing to hold ourselves accountable. I want all of us to experience the freedom and humility that comes from doing so.

Since no one is exempt from causing harm, acting like harm hasn't happened or there's a way we can somehow avoid or transcend it is a *red flag.* Be wary of anyone who sees themself above causing or repeating harm. Ideally we wouldn't need to be called into accountability by others or in ways so disruptive to our lives and bodies–when we possess shame resilience and a greater openness towards feedback surrounding the blind spots we can't see, but trust exist all the same, we will be more apt to recognize what belongs to us and take ownership and self-correct when needed.

When we feel more internal security we become the first ones running towards the community table, knowing that while we belong we are not entitled to sit and commune with anyone else feasting. We come humbly, knowing the fullness of who we are—we surrender with a mouthful of ownership because anything less than integrity tastes *awful,* it echoes shallowly, dully converts our magic to sawdust. We come volunteering our own name before anyone else feels the need to call us out–we confess our wrongdoing while still being connected to our dignity, we understand we may not always be able to make amends with others but are determined to lean in as best as we can and make things right with ourselves. Our sense of self-belonging hinges on it.

Third-way, reparative accountability has a specific goal, it aims for compassion-led transparency and a reset to safety for all involved. The path aligns with who we want to be, we pursue engagement with the practice before anyone has to expose us, knows about us, gives us an ultimatum or threatens us with consequences we can't live with or without–we do right by others because we first determine to do right by ourselves.

We are able to be a people led by self-accountability and integrity first and foremost, because we've spent enough time taking up residence inside our bodies and stories.

We've journeyed into the home of ourselves, exploring every closet within us previously barricaded, every dark room within us with lights turned off, every crevice of our foundation we assumed was cracked beyond repair. We've washed away the dead names, cobwebs and blessed the no-trespassing signs, for-sale signs and leftover misfitting keys others left behind before boarding the doors up. Shame, blame, regret and denial often mask themselves to appear like accountability however they will, without fail, return us to self-abandonment and a house of distorted mirrors.

We've learned to look into a clear mirror instead, unafraid of what's reflected back and, when in doubt, we look to people in our lives who are equally invested in our integrity and safety, trusting them to mirror back our truest selves and the parts we need to see and mature. We won't abandon or betray what we find since it belongs, *it all belongs.* We can love ourselves back to health, mature past a threshold of intolerance, and once again become safe enough to join others at the table.

We learn to meet ourselves with compassion because we witness in honesty our limits, knowing we'll stay the course and do the work—letting ourselves off the hook isn't an option our integrity affords. Seeing how far we've come already as a result of owning our flaws, missteps, ignorance and outright transgressions empowers us to anticipate and prepare ourselves for both more accountability and freedom. We trust ourselves and are determined to risk in the direction of who we want to be and become still.

I choose this and desire to integrate more third-way practices in my life through self-accountability—the ways I've harmed others will inevitably harm me too, no one is immune and no one walks away unscathed when we run from the truth of our lives.

Mel Gentry Bosna

We can repair with the magnetic hope that resetting to safety is possible and worth the risk—people are worth it, our integrity is worth it. I believe we can find a different way to care for ourselves and each other and this comes from witnessing the fullness of ourselves and remembering that we can face anything moving through dark waters. We can do this work, nothing will sink or drown us, I promise—lest you forget, you are the goddamn ocean.

Chapter Seven

CONSENT CULTURE

*"Anybody can walk amidst a hundred protestors, but to walk alone daily on the
path of humanity amidst inhumanity - that takes backbone."*

—Abhijit Naskar

"I think you can be even messier" were words my friend Gail texted me in
response to the section on white supremacy—she was referring to ways in which
she observes the inaction of white people as a paralysis stemming from
perfectionism, believing anti-racism has to be done the right way in order for it
to matter or involve less risk. Waiting until we know exactly what to say and do
is a set-up for ongoing harm, change won't effectively happen if we wait until
we feel perfectly equipped and ready to respond. Gail pointed to examples of
this in my own writing along with the ways she sees the fear of failure show up
in life. The crippling fear of criticism haunts many of us, restricting us from
trying, learning and repairing–it robs us of our full humanity and the
opportunities needed in order to build a better, safer world.

I've continued to draw her words in, holding them with curiosity because as soon as she sent the text my body recognized her words to be true. I've since been exploring ways it shows up in other parts of my life too, specifically how the presence of perfectionism might thwart efforts with creating consent culture.

It's hard enough to define what consent culture is let alone a path forward with *how* we might create one. I'm accepting there is not going to be any one way to do it nor a formula that can satisfy naming it either. I'm also accepting that because of how the world evolves, my understanding and practices will too, meaning I anticipate that after this book is published I will see the world differently and hopefully be owning and healing things in ways I can't foresee now. May we all continue pivoting as the direction of our path becomes clearer, may we let the direction change as continuously and often as it needs to. There's room to look back and say "I didn't know then what I know now–and now that I understand things differently I can show up differently and walk this path of repair differently." This is a practice in humility that propels us towards creating safety in our communities.

Chidimma Ozor Commer, licensed clinical social worker, therapist and researcher recently shared with me how every meeting she leads begins with addressing this necessary evolution and subsequent posture: *"Culture is always evolving and language is deeply tied to culture therefore our understanding of culture and use of language are necessarily evolving as well."* So should our anticipation and ownership of this progression—we can meet these changes and any mess involved with an open mind and posture.

Embodiment and self-reclamation practices don't come with a manual and it therefore seems important to acknowledge that building a safer world is no small, exact task. It is work that needs more of us awake, present, embodied, contributing in unique and collective ways.

In this same vein we can consider how building a consent culture *also* becomes a third-way path for us to explore, involving the messy middle of getting things wrong and flat-out-failing despite our best intentions. We risk this from humility because we're anchored to the desire for a safer world. We find a way to practice this messy middle together, willing to get things wrong and embrace what feels awkward, uncertain, and unfamiliar. By doing this we get to love each more wholly by holding firmly to lines that may feel newly delineated to parts of us, but that our bodies know with clarity must be drawn in order for more people to be held accountable.

Collective values vary from culture to culture in terms of what's considered admirable as well as what's judged as abhorrent. What we tolerate, justify, celebrate and reward reflect the societal, communal and spiritual values we are socialized within–sometimes these are consciously chosen however they are often values or beliefs we default to.

An overarching value I was raised with is the emphasis and prioritization of individualism. I remember a multitude of fragmented conversations I was exposed to in classrooms, around dinner tables and that were embedded in pop culture that reinforced the idea that everyone could achieve the white American dream if they worked hard enough and pulled themselves up by their own bootstraps. Success and failure were things we could independently earn and avoid if we were *just* smart enough, worked hard enough and were talented enough. Everyone could find their way to wealth and fame in the world. While empowering components of individualism exist, so do many vulnerabilities when individual power and personal gain are centered at the cost of the collective good. This imbalance allows for blanketed affirmation of individual success in addition to stigmatized rejection of individual failure.

When we default to individualism, we see the harm caused between people as solely being a result of 'personal issues' that don't have anything to do with us or our culture. This echoes in the defensive response commonly expressed in conversations on race which sound like *"Not all white people"* or similarly the response of *"Not all men"* in conversations about gendered violence. Individualism as a value quickly sees violent behavior as indicative of people who are outliers–the lone wolf trope acting out of isolation. The distance individualism creates between collective safety and personal responsibility is a dangerous blind spot.

When individual behaviors are centered we assume people are in categories of being either good *or* bad, which sets up all involved for ongoing harm. When this happens we end up distancing ourselves from behaviors that need to be addressed and people who need to own their part and also heal–or as Kelly aptly shared in the last chapter, we *"Eject people from community"* as a means of securing safety. However boundaries alone without inner work will not necessarily produce a safer world, we all remain vulnerable to repeating the same behaviors elsewhere. No one wins.

We *absolutely* need and deserve boundaries to ensure individual and collective safety. Reparative accountability is a third-way, non-binary path that can help us travel towards our integrity when we lose our way. It has the power to reset us as individuals and the potential to reset our relationships and community to a place of increased safety and stability. However when we practice boundaries without healing the wounded parts underneath the violation we may continue to feel a sense of fear, shame and isolation. I want to explore what it might look like to create and uphold cultural practices of internal and external consent.

I've been working with Trey for a few months and today he is visibly shaking on my office couch.

"I have something I need to say."

He's been prone to anxiety throughout his life however the energy I'm observing with his body today feels different, nearly frenetic. I quickly assess the session is about to pivot into a confessional experience and since I am neither an investigator nor a priest, I ask him to please pause, slow down, breathe with me. I'm concerned that whatever he's about to disclose may actually cause him harm, something doesn't seem right about the timing—healing *does* require taking ownership of our stories and responsibility for our actions. Growth requires vulnerability and can feel very disruptive and risky, however when we rush into it or force ourselves past our own window of tolerance, we may end up violating our internal consent and harm the parts of us that aren't yet ready or willing. This is often what contributes to feeling emotionally flooded.

While co-regulating with him, I start to share how I'm here, ready and willing to support him however his body language is telling me there are parts of him that don't appear to be consenting to sharing things with me—or are afraid of what will happen once they do. I start to feel our breath sync, his body is settling and then he abruptly starts trembling again—before I can say anything further he blurts out *"I used to touch my cousin."*

144

A House Restored

He can't make eye contact with me and I recognize he's afraid he'll see in me the disgust he feels towards himself. Having had months of therapy sessions with him before this moment, I assess that part of him confessed for absolution, a part that is so very tired of suffering—another part of him is likely disclosing though as an act of self-harm. If I reject him in the way he's rejected himself, if I shame him the way he shames himself, then part of him will experience confirmation of what he fears and already believes, which is to say that he's an awful human being who deserves torment.

"Hey."

I pause for a moment, waiting, keeping my breath steady, encouraging him to sync his breathing with mine again—he continues staring at the floor and I sense the border of a panic attack surfacing.

"Trey–hey–I understand this is going to feel *really* scary, I wonder though, can you hear my voice and possibly look at me? Can you find my eyes?"

I exhale deeply and hope my face mirrors the compassion I feel towards this part of him that's horrifically entangled in perpetual shame and suffering. I mean the words that follow even though there's also a part of me who, as a survivor, feels activated too.

"Thank you for trusting me. I'm still here."

Trey met my eyes, the liminal tension between us an invitation to allow a third-way path to emerge. No person heals from an exiled state of self-hatred. In the same way humans can't evolve without encountering compassion, reparative accountability and encountering our humanity, *culture won't change either*.

We're not going to change culture effectively without finding a third-way. As long as we polarize our beliefs and identities and engage in dualistic approaches, we will be unable to be with ourselves and in turn, diminish how much consent we can actually access and practice with those around us. We delay cultural change when we only have extreme options presented that either don't resonate or feel in conflict with who we are.

The messy middle of owning and repairing our participation in the world is how I see us moving forward.

Mel Gentry Bosna

Frustration and grief are common feelings I encounter when reading the news, while listening to human tragedy and when navigating places of pain in my own life. Some of this frustration is derived from the lack of self-accountability and vulnerability we encounter from those in power. It has led me to practice greater curiosity as to why so many people profess a desire towards growth and yet cycle in patterns of behavior and avoidance preventing us collectively from moving forward into it.

From my perspective there are two cardinal emotions which seem to fuel our avoidance with being in our bodies. These emotions commandeer the exposure of our stories which exist *underneath* our harmful behaviors: fear, a primal and necessary human stress response that aids in survival, and shame, a primary threat to human belonging.

From an evolutionary, biological lens, fear has aided our continued existence in necessary ways, allowing both humans and animals increased chances of survival. Fear itself is one of our primary emotions, connecting us to our need for safety—in fact *all human emotions are purposeful* and point us towards our needs. The following description is an over-simplification yet worth considering nonetheless: loneliness surfaces when we have an unmet need for connection, anger surfaces when there are injustices and boundary violations, sadness emerges when we need comfort and soothing, guilt aligns us with our need to repair, take responsibility and be realigned with our integrity.

Emotions are part of our necessary makeup and learning how to *be with* our emotions is critical so we can better attune to our needs and underlying wounds. This is how we reclaim more of ourselves and mature into discerning what are actual threats to fear compared to what we've been socialized or manipulated to fear instead.

Shame on the other hand isn't an evolutionary response however it is tied to one of our primary human needs–it's different from guilt even though the two are often conflated. Guilt is feeling bad about something we've done whereas shame is feeling bad about *who we are*. Guilt is an emotion that can wake us up, shame is an experience that shuts us down. Regret can be a response to guilt when it comes from our truest self, pivoting us from self-punishment instead towards self-ownership, allowing us to repair what we did from humility and reemerge.

It might sound something along these lines: "*I regret so deeply I acted that way–it's so far from who I want to be and actually know myself to be–I hate that I harmed you and am committed to doing better. What do you need from me?*"

Guilt and regret *can* catapult us towards ourselves when we have enough shame-resilience to face ourselves honestly and, in response, care for the parts of us struggling. This process has the power to reconnect us to our values. On the other hand, the drowning weight of shame says our struggles are *who* we are—we acted badly because we are bad. When we don't have enough of an internal structure around our worth nor developed enough shame resilience, guilt can devolve into shame and we become blended with it.

The younger we are when we experience shame, the less internal structure of self we have as it takes time and safe experience to develop. This is why many of us continue in patterns of feeling worthless into adulthood, seeing ourselves as broken. We spend our lives avoiding being seen for who we ashamedly believe ourselves to be and can neither experience personal healing nor participate in repairing harm we've caused others.

Where fear operates from our needs related to survival, shame is activated from either an internalized belief of being bad or someone else's displaced interpretation that *how we survived* now makes us bad. Fear may tell us to do whatever it takes to survive whereas shame uses a whip to condemn us for what we did in order to survive—it's from the bridged tension between terror and self-condemnation that we abandon ourselves, betray our values and trespass the boundaries and consent of others. We cyclically survive, exist and self-deteriorate when we inhabit this space instead of the home our body was safely meant for us to embody. From shame we can only offer empty consent to others because we aren't home with ourself *as our truest self.*

Due to binary and dualistic frameworks offered of either being a *good* or *bad* person we are quick then to fall deep into shame or just as dangerous, reject appropriate guilt as a way of trying to manage feelings and bypass our discomfort. This leads us further away from repair. The irony of all of it being how many of us actually remain in shame because of how much we *actually, deeply value* having integrity—we think the only way forward is to continue punishing ourselves as a way of making sure we take responsibility for our actions. This, however, is not a practice of self-accountability but one of punitive, self-punishment. Many feel like it's somehow necessary to drown in shame believing it's the only way to make our wrong-doing right.

This could not be further than the truth–no one wins when shame is a decision maker. Not only does it leave us feeling like we're drowning, it doesn't provide actual repair for others which only becomes possible when we take responsibility for ourselves and practice a third-way accountability. When we can't engage in repair we cannot individually or collectively reset to safety. Shame inevitably isolates us from ourselves and others, it's the absence of safety, the furthest island away from home.

Everyone deserves better—and I say this with an intense conviction to see the world hold itself to a higher standard—I don't believe it's possible to become safer when we stay blended with shame and I don't think we *can* repair harm unless we come back to our body and integrity.

Shame, fear and the subsequent desperation that follows distorts our ability to judge what's best for ourselves and others—these emotions hijack consent. In order to practice embodied consent we have to have options other than disconnecting from ourselves or being labeled and rejected as social pariahs, irredeemable outcasts no longer worthy of being part of a community. We need a culture and more importantly, a community, that allows us to find our way back to our humanity when we step outside of who we want and need to be–and we need to know how to offer each other a way back to health while still practicing whatever boundaries are necessary to keep ourselves and others safe in the process. This is the messy middle, this is where we learn to come home together and how we build a more vibrant world.

Years ago I was introduced to self-compassion expert, researcher and professor Dr. Kristen Neff. Her work introduced a counter-culture approach with how to practice self-compassion and gain perspective with how to see ourselves outside of failure and vulnerability which we're either prone to avoid or fixate on. Her work was a catalyst for providing a transformative shift with how I approach the rougher edges of my humanity, and what I'm able to now extend to others regarding skills development. If we start with a foundational perspective that rejects a binary lens of being either good *or* bad and instead embrace how all humans are varying degrees of good, bad and average-in-between, space develops to practice curiosity and compassion around the parts of us worthy of celebrating and the parts of us in need of growth.

A few years after finding Kristen Neff's book '*Self-Compassion*', I was introduced to a therapeutic model called *Internal Family Systems* (IFS) created by Richard Schwartz. IFS also felt radically counter-culture and simultaneously wholly resonate with the ways I experience being human. The model assumes we are all many parts and that *each part of us belongs*—it's when we reject a part of us instead of including it that we risk disconnection, dissociation, compartmentalization and wind up feeling stuck in wounds and behaviors we feel powerless to. Problems arise not from having parts but from trying to get rid of them.

The IFS framework which affirms humans have many parts, none of which are bad, empowers us to individually and collectively explore what needs to be called-in, soothed, addressed, owned and transformed. If I assume there is no such category as being good *or* bad then there is no need to react, reject or shame myself nor anyone else into doing better. Shame is an effective tool of coercion but not an effective path for transformation.

Patriarchy, religious fundamentalism and white supremacy hijack consent development and rely on binary, dualistic language and identifiers–us/them, good/bad, black/white, innocent/guilty. Many people with good intentions appear hesitant or unwilling to explore what parts exist inside our bodies and stories that may be benefiting from systems that perpetuate harm. This avoidance ensures on-going participation in systems that do not reflect our values, it's harmful towards others and ourselves.

As I've sat with Trey in my office this year it's been apparent he too is familiar with the cultural, communal and family dynamics we've been exploring. When he violated his cousin he was himself also a child and one whom I'd assess had also been violated. Growing up he wasn't presented with many choices about who he was allowed to be nor how to get help when he needed it. His family structure was strict, rigid, traditional—the religious practices they were involved in dominated his childhood.

Mel Gentry Bosna

When we first began exploring the dynamics around what brought him to therapy it was clear he felt stuck somewhere between self-judgment and self-punishment, he couldn't see a path out of suffering. Trey wanted relief but had already been handed the roll of judge, jury and executioner due to how he'd been raised to believe he was intrinsically bad. He'd been taught to believe that the only way to becoming good was through god's redemption–a god mind you, whom he'd also been raised to believe saw him as an abomination.

When Trey left fundamentalism he remained stuck with feeling powerless as the only path to restoration he'd seen modeled was one where he'd have to lay down his life, reject his sexuality and submit to a god and religious system incongruent with his deepest self. Perhaps this seems extreme however as a clinician who works with survivors of religious abuse, it's a frequent experience I hear others process.

Most the men I've worked with, whether straight, cis, trans, queer, religious or having had no spiritual upbringing whatsoever—share variations of the same options from their childhood. Either the message from their communities was to abandon their power due to how dangerous and out of control they were *or* to dominate others with their power since others' emotionality made them less trustworthy and weak. One is rooted in a shame response and the other is motivated by fear.

When all we see modeled in the systems and leadership around us are responses rooted in fear, shame and coercion, the options for male goodness disappear and one becomes either prey *or* predator, victim *or* conqueror, lion *or* sacrificial lamb, good guy *or* bad guy. Within the structure of toxic masculinity the conqueror becomes the *only* valid option for belonging. When I have conversations about toxic masculinity with men I often observe them filter what shared through a fear of vulnerability and anticipated castration. It seems what's often interpreted is that *men* are dangerous when what I'm actually naming is the dangers of toxic masculinity for everyone, including *men.*

In order to develop a culture of consent we have to create ways for humans to return to relational belonging and safety when we stray from our integrity and cause harm *and* we must simultaneously create boundaries, enforce natural consequences and defer to the needs and discernment of the individuals and communities harmed and who remain vulnerable. Whoever has caused harm does not determine when they've done enough repair for others to feel safe. We need a path for all parties involved to find a way back to their humanity and a way forward with becoming restored and valued.

Whether people hold themselves accountable or take opportunities presented to them to heal is something we cannot control, however it's an invitation we can offer that embodies the reparative power to reset our communities to safety. Developing community practices that extend options *outside of* prematurely welcoming someone back into a relationship, restoring them rashly to positions of power *or* ejecting them permanently from community as an irredeemable threat will undoubtedly be messy. Without these options however, we will perpetually engage in empty consent from parts of us either afraid or ashamed which keeps harm activated in our bodies and communities.

People often presume the way to build a safer world is through changing others' beliefs or controlling their behaviors. This is problematic, vulnerable and arrogant in that it assumes certain beliefs are superior to others. I think a better option is to explore the underlying reasons we don't always access or live from our core values. What might the world look like if we trusted and supported one another instead of trying to control each other? What if we did more of our own inner work and lived with less fear and shame, could we trust more freely individuals and communities to self-govern? Our beliefs are clearly important however when we're in crisis our trauma responses are significantly more likely to influence how we react, especially if we don't feel safe enough to have or explore all our options.

I know from personal experience how likely we are to deviate from personal beliefs when fear and shame are present, *no matter how strong our beliefs and convictions may otherwise be.*

When I was twenty-one years old I identified as politically conservative, and, uncoincidentally, religiously devout and conventionally pro-life. Even all these decades later my body still remembers how it felt to stand in a tiny bathroom holding my first pregnancy test knowing full well that my belief of human life beginning at conception would not be enough to stop me from getting an abortion.

I'd been raised to think of abortion as murder and while my religious community and family may have offered exceptions to abortion in cases of rape or incest those were taboo topics no one explored with me, so I grew up with a rigid concept about body autonomy. Which is to say that when it came to sex and pregnancy I did not see my body as belonging to me. It first belonged to god and secondly belonged to men.

In this same season I volunteered at a local crisis pregnancy center, facilitating pregnancy tests for other girls and women—the seeming hypocrisy of this doesn't escape me, however I also don't imagine my experience of 'helping' others in a situation I found myself in was all that uncommon. Thus far this had been my only experience with those little death-grip-life-changing-sticks. While I waited the three minutes for my results to emerge, I remember feeling certain even then that despite how unequivocally pro-life and anti-abortion I was during that season, there would have been no alternative way out of the desperation that was steadily increasing inside of me each minute that I waited. I did not feel like I had valid options to choose from, felt terrified, ashamed and suddenly understood how many reasons could exist for abortion.

What good are our beliefs, convictions and certainties when we can't access compassion for how often desperation drives how we live, survive and suffer the ways in which we do. Due to binary options of either being good *or* bad, either for *or* against each other, we become threatened when we or others struggle and are therefore unable to see the whole of our humanity. Often, we are more invested in condemning each other to live brittle stories in isolation than we are in the wellbeing of our communities.

Pregnancy, potential or otherwise, has always held various layers of compacted emotion for me. I remember the unexpected pregnancy that happened when I was thirty, two months after I gave birth to my first child—how hard I sobbed because I didn't want another baby yet—how weeks later I miscarried and found myself sobbing from both guilt and relief, perhaps feeling guilty *because* of the relief. Two years later I became pregnant intentionally after months of trying, when I began bleeding during the first trimester I felt so scared of losing that pregnancy. Every time following that I heard the sounds fetal activity made I cried, it was precious to me. I've wept for many different reasons around pregnancy and can't help but grieve that we live in a vulnerable, polarized world where many of us have so few people to weep in front of due to fear, shame and the complexity of our experiences.

I tried reconciling an ideology I was raised to believe with a reality I couldn't have lived out as a tender-ache of a young woman. I stood in that bathroom feeling very alone. I didn't want an abortion nor did I want to become a mother. The dread of facing my community and family easily outweighed any alternative option otherwise considered. The options we feel we can access are the *only* ones that carry actual weight in the moment. Regardless of how many well-meaning arguments are made on the behalf of other options, if they aren't experienced as safe and valid by the body they are more often than not options we elect to choose from. Ironically, neither the option of terminating nor carrying the pregnancy to term would've been an option I was consenting to from *self*, both were filtered through my stress responses of fear and shame.

Whenever I've shared publicly about this season of my life I've purposefully allowed ambiguity to surround whether I had an abortion or not—I am neither ashamed nor afraid, my vagueness is intentional. My hope has been to have more people join in with exploring the messy middle of third-way exploration. Rather than fixate solely on outcomes, perhaps we care for our communities' underlying needs and vulnerabilities more holistically, consider the process of where and why we often feel alone.

Why bring this up in a chapter on consent culture? Because having reproductive rights, body autonomy and the agency to choose what's in alignment with our values and needs has *everything* to do with practicing consent collectively. If we want to reduce abortions that occur due to an overwhelm of fear, shame and desperation, then having options that resource and empower individuals and communities with affordable, accessible healthcare, parental care, childcare and quality education are the standards for how we can better honor each other.

Comprehensive and holistic options are the *bare minimum* of building a consent culture—having agency and body autonomy are not enough if we don't feel safe enough to access choices even *if* they are available.

Empty consent occurs from two distinct vulnerabilities, the first of which is disconnection from ourselves–when we're not present and attuned enough to our bodies we may not know our desires, needs and limitations and our expressed '*yes, no and maybe*' is an echo from unawareness. Secondly, many of us practice empty consent even when we *do* know what's happening inside us, however due to shame, fear or desperation, our expressed '*yes, no and maybe*' arises out of our reaction to avoid harm. How many of us have engaged in empty consent somewhere in our lives? Hint: the answer is all of us.

Choice in itself is not enough to guarantee outcome yet having choice is a fundamental part of consent and safety—without choices we are at war either within ourselves or with each other. Without safety we cannot consent internally nor relationally, meaning we are chronically engaged in self-abandonment and dissociation. Choice is fundamental to consent culture, there is no other way around this—removing agency will always result in supremacy structures and 'power-over' approaches. I cannot stress it enough: it harms us all.

I am invested in reducing the number of unwanted pregnancies and abortions that occur in the world in the same way I am invested in safe, whole communities where we better love our neighbors and help each other lay our weapons down.

We can and must have agency and safety to access ourselves more fully if we want more people to make decisions from integrity, intuition, and most importantly, from the deep well of our shared humanity. Changing culture must involve a dialectical framework of both/and, meaning change is blocked from happening unless we recognize both our individual AND collective responsibility to engage and rights to self-govern. We won't be able to bring about transformative cultural change unless more of us are willing to show up to the often-awkward, messy middle ground of doing the right thing with an understanding how often we'll get it wrong as one right path doesn't exist—either way we cannot know how to better love the world without more risk.

We are only able to practice and explore a middle way if we become more embodied, meaning, integrity and dignity only direct our behaviors and decisions if our bodies are settled and safe to intuit what's in alignment. Otherwise we are apt to filter and react to the world through shame and fear.

Choice is a prerequisite to consent.

Consent is a prerequisite to safety.

Safety is a prerequisite to healing.

Embodiment is the foundation of being able to access all of the above.

The majority of us want sexual violence to decrease in our communities—many of us are also committed to reducing abortions, poverty, domestic violence, hunger, addiction, mass shootings, incarceration rates, racial inequity, gendered violence and transphobic hate crimes. To reduce harm we must pivot from conflict into embodiment. Our communities experience more safety when we hold *ourselves* to a higher standard of accountability and center our shared, innate dignity. Owning our part feels good, deeply worth it—we call ourselves into wholeness before someone else calls us out of it. Prioritizing repair over reputation, abundance over scarcity, integrity over individualism becomes a life rhythm we move freely within.

Building consent culture involves respecting the boundaries and rights of others to exist safely and fully as they are. Verbal commitment parallels the problem previously named with prioritizing 'good intentions', meaning that while commitment matters it remains empty without transformative action backing it up. Intentions are hollow without ownership of impact and they remain empty when our character and actions don't evolve.

Laura McKowen's words are the generative energy we bring to changing culture, "*You cannot do it alone and only you can do it.*" We get to embrace the messy middle of building a new path through third-way practices, we cannot do it perfectly and we cannot do it alone and we can and must risk differently if we want to create a safer world.

Chapter Eight

HOMEBODIED: AN ONGOING PRACTICE

"My love language is sending you back to yourself."

–Maryam Hasnaa

He looked down and then to his left before looking at me, exhaling a deep breath and furrowing his brow. I had to fight an urge to rub my index finger on the screen and relax his eyebrow muscles—this was a virtual therapy session taking place via telehealth. Henry is a newer client to my practice, we'd begun exploring his avoidance of certain emotions and I'd just asked if he could locate where he felt anger in his body.

His eyebrows were communicating as much to me as the words that followed, *"What do you mean where do I feel it?"*

Embodiment is a deep, endless well I love to draw from, I smile and reply. "Emotions surface as relevant data, pointing us toward parts of our bodies which hold needs and wounds—think of your feelings as one of many sacred expressions that carry a message to tune towards. Our bodies house the story until we're ready to retell it, holding it on our behalf."

He takes a shaky breath, *"I'm afraid to feel my anger, what if I hurt someone with it—what if I hurt HER with it."*

I validate how, when things are unfamiliar, they *do* feel risky—in fact more often than not we think of unfamiliar things as unsafe when the reality is many of us are stuck in patterns and behaviors that feel familiar but are compromising our sense of well-being alongside our safety and those we most love around us.

"It's true Henry—you *could* hurt someone with the way you express your anger…but also what if instead you could feel your anger in a way that healed what hurt and actually made her feel safer too? Avoiding it doesn't seem to be working."

This is a chapter about deepening our embodied consent *skills* practice—here is how we walk onto new ground and do this holy work together.

A foundational layer with practicing embodied consent relates to our ability to feel, express *and* regulate our emotions. Many of us are never shown how to be with big feelings without seeing dissociation or dysregulation modeled. If the adults present in our childhood dismissed our feelings or shut us down all together by reacting with big emotions of their own, it would've been difficult to learn how to feel, express and regulate our emotions. Kids aren't supposed to know how to cope with emotions or express themselves—many adults sadly never learn either.

In order to practice consent we need access to our internal compass, in order to have access we learn how to be with the emotions and thoughts happening inside us in a way we are unintimidated by them—we become intimately familiar with the internal landscape of our history.

In addition to building confidence around our own experience, emotion regulation skills are crucial to consent practice as they help us feel safer being around *others'* emotions and reactions. These skills empower our bodies to process emotion without experiencing them as threatening. Not only do we need to be able to hear our own inner *'yes, no and maybe'*, we need to be able to receive others' responses as well.

When we don't know how to handle the boundaries expressed by others or the emotions that surface within us as a result, we're prone to default to a stress response (fight, flight, freeze, flock or fawn). While there will always be instances when a stress response remains our safest or most accessible option we ideally want to discern as many choices for ourselves as possible, emotion regulation skills and embodiment practices are what grant us greater ability to stay present in our body.

While the structure of rape culture is upheld by institutional systems of power there are also layers inside each of us which perpetuate violent culture, namely the degrees to which we're emotionally fragile, feel entitled or lack the skills we need in order to communicate and meet our needs appropriately. For instance, one reason many people don't

communicate their feelings or set boundaries is due to fear of how others' will react to their boundary. If we want others to feel safe around us we need to develop skills to regulate our emotions and reactions. We need to know how to process disappointment or anger when someone sets a boundary with *us*, we need to know how to hear the word 'no'. Navigating disappointment, anger, hurt and rejection is critical with building consent culture. Behaviors are not expressed in isolation—behaviors are data, symptoms of underlying vulnerabilities, emotions and unmet needs.

The number of conversations I've had with women and non-binary people who've resorted to having *bad sex they didn't want to have* in order to try and avoid a violent sexual assault is TOO MANY–the fear of someone's reaction to hearing *'no'* was a theme that dominated the conversations I had with research participants.

We need to equip kids and adolescents with the ability to regulate their emotions, hear other's boundaries and navigate situations where consent is unclear or is withdrawn—we need a generation of adults who practice giving and receiving consent and are becoming attuned to the ways consent may be accessed differently for those with less structural power.

Mel Gentry Bosna

These practices are rooted in a significantly deeper understanding than what the majority of us are taught about consent, namely that the absence of a person's 'no' somehow implies a 'yes.' The reality is, often when a clear '*no, yes and maybe*' has not been expressed, we are receiving data that the person answering may need more time, permission or safety in order to express what they want or need.

This doesn't apply exclusively to sex—how many of us agree to social events, family plans, school activities, work demands, etc. despite having part of us clearly hesitant to engage or commit. How many times have we been coerced or pressured into doing something socially we haven't wanted–or hell, how many of us have upgraded to a membership plan that we don't need or want simply because we don't know how to say 'no' or are worried about being harassed by another for doing so. Without wanting to over-generalize people-pleasing and codependency, it's clear enough to see this as a stress response strongly related to fear of others' reactions for expressing needs, feelings and boundaries.

As a result of not knowing *how* to navigate our emotions and others' reactions while trying to be a decent human people are comfortable being around—or hell, minimally not seen as an asshole—many of us act in similar patterns to Henry's. We avoid our feelings and needs hoping they eventually go away or somehow become less important. The intention of avoidance is to reduce harm however the impact of avoiding our needs, emotions and boundaries inevitably leads to greater disruption.

In the long run avoidance develops into patterns with self-abandonment and an increase in unmet needs and big emotions—when we ignore our internal world, our desperation to feel seen and heard has no other option but to come out sideways, bigger than intended. We harm both others and ourselves in the process.

We cannot heal what we're not willing to incrementally feel, cannot practice embodied consent when cut off from parts of ourselves, cannot handle others' emotions and boundaries when we feel overwhelmed by them or entitled to their compliance. What follows is a loose road map to practice curiosity with, I'd invite you to explore the following skills and practices which support a more present way of being. Imagine a world where more of us live connected to our core selves, knowing and trusting our expansiveness and capability of being present with our emotions and memories–it sends goosebumps up and down my

160

body! Imagine a world safe enough to express our limits, needs and boundaries without fear of being ejected from community, the threat of physical or sexual violence or the loss of love and belonging. I can sense it–and even when I doubt whether I'll see more of it in my lifetime, I believe humans deserve more safety, belonging and autonomy.

I've lovingly started referring to people with embodiment practices and access to their inner compass as *homebodied.* May these skills provide you direction with finding your way back inward, may you welcome more of yourself home than ever before in your practice.

SKILLS FOR ACCESSING INTERNAL CONSENT CREATING AN EMBODIMENT PRACTICE

BREATH WORK
I can't emphasize enough how important knowing how to access and use breath is when our bodies get activated. Breathing from the chest has been shown to have the potential impact of inducing a panic or anxiety attack. We want to be able to slow our breath, steadily breathing from our belly and focusing on our exhale which communicates to our limbic and nervous systems that we're safe. This in turn allows us more executive functioning to discern how to return to safety if/when needed. Breathing while using grounding skills for orientation of time, place and options is foundational.

GROUNDING SKILLS
Different people prefer varying types of skills for grounding the body when flooded by emotions or memories, and to the degree that you find yourself triggered you may need different types of skills and support. Grounding skills involve using the body's five senses and breath, helping us orient to time and place. Chapter 4 included the 5-4-3-2-1 grounding skills technique to help orient Jade to the room and present moment. This helped settle her nervous system, allowing her body to shift into a calmer, more neutral state, which in turn then

allowed access to a different perspective and additional skills that would otherwise have been unavailable if she had dissociated or become emotionally flooded. Other grounding skills include breathing techniques, guided muscle relaxation, movement, distraction, humor, drumming, gardening and sensory play to name a few. It's not uncommon to need support sometimes while grounding–when the body and stress levels become more acutely activated we all benefit from relational support.

EMOTION REGULATION SKILLS

Emotion regulating skills traditionally help us tolerate the reactions our bodies have with either real or perceived threat along with any emotional waves or body sensations that might feel temporarily intolerable. However, tolerance feels like the bare-minimum goal to attain–I prefer we find ways to dial down the intensity of our emotions and body sensations with the purpose of containment until we have greater capacity to heal and care for whatever wound is being bumped.

This is why I emphasize consent-based body approaches that allow us to titrate our emotions in a way that feels safe enough to be with–my clients frequently laugh, roll their eyes or flip me off due to how often I bring up incremental emotional processing and containment or distract them with some seemingly benign or ridiculous topic to help them ground and down-shift into regulating an emotion that seconds before seemed unimaginable to be with and talk about. They don't necessarily *like* that the work is incremental due to wanting relief from pain sooner and yet gain understanding over time as to why incremental processing is effective with aiding regulation, containment and emotional release without destabilizing them in the process.

INTERNAL FAMILY SYSTEMS / PARTS WORK

As previously mentioned, Internal Family Systems or as it's commonly referred to, IFS, is a therapeutic modality which can be an effective way of learning how to be with parts of ourselves in distress without becoming overwhelmed by them. Whenever I encounter my own hesitation, resistance, fear–essentially any BIG feeling–I practice seeing it as a part of me present to communicate a need or emotion–if it's only one part of us then we can turn towards it with curiosity, care and the support it needs. Without un-blending from an activated part we increase our vulnerability of defaulting to empty consent. IFS can be utilized independently or with a guide such as a therapist who has been trained in it. Richard Schwartz's book *No Bad Parts* is a great jumping off point.

CURIOSITY & SELF-COMPASSION
Sometimes a part of us shows up loudly with a definitive "HELL NO" and other times it shows up as a gentle hesitation, a part reluctant to move forward. Regardless of how a part shows up, a gift we can give ourselves is an intentional pause so we can practice more curiosity and compassion towards whatever part of us feels threatened, has a boundary in need of being reinforced or has a different request for safety. The neurotransmitter in our brain that's released as we practice curiosity, whether with ourselves or others, is dopamine which overtime increases self-alignment and helps stabilize our mood and behaviors rather than increasing self-abandonment and self-judgment. We can trust that as we practice curiosity and compassion towards our big emotions, reactions and triggers, that we'll eventually gain more access to what's going on underneath and what we in turn need.

An example of this in my own life happens when I'm watching the news and start to notice my body's reaction to whatever truly terrible thing is happening in the world. Previously I might've found myself blended with feelings of anxiety or overwhelm about the state of things—oftentimes as a result my body would respond in panic by either feeling helpless (Freeze response), immediately wanting to post something on social media (Flock response) or a dive into action in order to rescue others from said horrible situation and myself from anxiety and guilt (mix of Fight and Fawn responses along with white saviorism).

Instead, when I notice my body becoming activated by the news I now try to drop into my body and breath, practice curiosity about what's coming up for me, what parts are feeling emotions and now respond to them with gentle inquiry and compassion-led questions. It's from there—a settled place rather than a stressed response that I can then reengage with the world outside me and do better, be better, live better.

BODY-BASED/INTUITIVELY LED ACTIVITIES
The list here could be endless! Basically any activity that helps you practice being *in* your body, *with* your body and that invites curiosity, pleasure and calm. Examples include building practices around intuitive eating, joyful movement, yoga, massage, erotic expression, massage, gardening, appropriate risk-taking,

energy work, dancing, drumming, being in nature and *so much more*. Whatever makes you feel ALIVE and is within your values, boundaries, integrity and need for safety can work to help you feel more embodied and emboldened with being yourself.

BODY/SOMATIC CENTERED THERAPY
A therapeutic option includes utilizing a clinician trained in somatic modalities who could support your practice with getting back into your body, the site where our stories, history, emotions and wounds are stored. A therapist who specializes in this might have training in Somatic Experience (SE), Brain-Spotting, Internal Family Systems, breathwork, sound baths, sand tray and guided meditation to name a few.

Cognitive Behavioral Therapy, Acceptance Commitment Therapy and EMDR are common therapeutic modalities which are often effective with certain situations and needs however are considered top-down approaches with treating trauma, meaning they start cognitively in thought or memory and move down into the body.

The somatic modalities previously mentioned are considered *bottom-up* approaches, originating from the body and moving upward towards cognitive reprocessing. *All* these methods can be helpful depending on individual needs presenting–clinically I defer to body-based approaches more often than not, trusting the wisdom of our body's containment and power. It all belongs, what's most important is discovering what aligns for your needs in the season you're in.

A resonate quote I often return to by writer and scholar Ehime Ora reads:

> *You gotta resurrect the deep pain within you and give it a place to live that's not within your body. Let it live in art. Let it live in writing. Let it live in music. Let it be devoured by building brighter connections. Your body is not a coffin for pain to be buried in. Put it somewhere else.*

A House Restored

ONGOING EDUCATION

There exist a wealth of educational resources on toxic masculinity, anti-racism engagement, deconstructing religious fundamentalism, boundaries, codependency, reclamation and relational work. Dismantle the systems of power that are embedded inside you, specifically rape culture and white supremacy frameworks which allow power to pretend to be on the good side of the game. A list of resources for consideration and vetting can be found on my website.

Stay engaged, decolonize your bookshelves, listen and *pay* non-white and non-cis/male educators who are not the default voices of power. Commit to an open-mind, remain a student and take ownership of your own education, reclamation and personal growth practices. If you have financial means and connections, provide educational opportunities for others in your community–not as a leader but as a bridge–ensure the original people who labored are credited and compensated accordingly.

RELATIONAL & COMMUNITY SKILL PRACTICES

In an ideal *(ahem,* fantasy?) world we'd possess all the internal skills we needed before practicing them with others, and, that's not the realm we live in nor is it the way many of us actually learn the way our own compass navigates *let alone* how to honor the needs and boundaries of others. It's a non-dualistic, dialectical practice of both/and meaning we practice listening and honoring our internal *'yes, no and maybe'* while also learning how to navigate and honor the external *'yes, no and maybe'* consent practices of other people. This is how toddlers and children would also ideally and most effectively learn too–through safe experience. The next set of skills are specifically related to relational practice in conjunction and in alignment with individual practice.

OPEN-ENDED CONVERSATION

Learn how to ask about someone's needs, preferences and boundaries in a way that allows for something other than binary responses. When we ask close-ended questions we are reducing a person's response to a singular part and one that might be expressed without safety, awareness or pleasure. Notice the difference between these closed-ended and open-ended questions: *"Do you like this?"* compared to *"What would feel good right now?"* or alternatively, *"What are things that currently feel off limits that I can respect?"*

Consider the difference even with these two open-ended questions: "*What are your non-negotiables?*" compared to "*I understand that what feels okay can change depending on the people involved and the specific situation and feelings involved, so I won't assume this is a blanket response–what would feel okay for you right now, I don't want to go any further until we both feel on-board.*"

Or, in a context that perhaps isn't sexual, consider the differences between these questions: "*I really want us to be together for Mother's Day this year, can you come at 11AM?*" compared to this alternative response, "*It'd mean a lot to me for us to be together for Mother's Day but I know that you have other people to consider and it's also your only day off–I'd like to get together around 11AM but want to hear your thoughts about what would also work for you*" or even this one, "*What are everyone's thoughts about Mother's Day this year? I'd always love to see you but know there are other needs that deserve consideration.*"

Ask with openness and curiosity about others' feelings and needs and if it remains unclear, defer to being led rather than leading based on power differentials. For instance, if you're a cisgender, straight man and you're uncertain whether the person you're with is clearly consenting, do not infer if they are, become aware and defer to the power dynamics in the room; follow the lead of the person you're with or share your concern that you're having difficulty discerning what is actually desired and safe.

PRACTICE WITH OTHERS
I cannot stress the importance of practicing these skills within relationships which, ironically, is where many of us avoid our work due to the anticipation of getting things wrong, overreacting or repeating an old pattern. Consider starting by identifying a few people who feel 'safe enough' to be 'vulnerable enough' to practice with–perhaps name your intention in advance for the purpose of support and accountability (i.e. that you're wanting to work on setting boundaries, expressing your needs, feeling disappointed/hearing a 'no' response, etc.) Ideally we practice giving and receiving consent and boundaries where it feels safer so that in situations that involve more tension or the presence of a stress response, the skills are more familiar and accessible. There are plenty of great books on boundary work, keep learning and practicing with them!

EXPERIMENT WITH THREE OR MORE OPTIONS

This is not a hard and fast rule, however when stepping outside of all-or-nothing, dualistic thinking, it's helpful to make sure we have a minimum of three options to choose from. When there are only two available we may end up defaulting into the old familiarity of empty consent (choosing the lesser of two things we don't want). When we have more than two options it can feel energetically more in alignment and as though we're actually choosing what we want or need. Same goes for practice with others–consider giving a couple of options to others to choose from and especially within the framework of open-ended questions that allow for input or curiosity for another response to be explored.

PRACTICING SELF-ACCOUNTABILITY WITH OTHERS

This looks like volunteering where you goofed, recognized you need feedback or outright participated in harm. Perhaps it's letting someone know they crossed a boundary or initiating a conversation where you're checking in to see if you've crossed someone else's boundary (ideally before they have to confront you). Ask people how they feel around you or if there are things that you could work on to help them feel more safe. Take responsibility for your actions and energy whenever you see that you've stepped outside your integrity or participated in harm, include a plan for what you're working on and be open to hearing what others may need from you instead. Offer yourself and others permission slips that create room for change and evolution, for changing your mind, your plans or the way you used to approach things, etc.

PRACTICING EMBODIMENT IN CONFLICT AND STRESS

This skill goes back to our practices of breathwork, grounding, self-soothing and regulating our emotions in situations that feel tense, stressful and full-on triggering. It's important to practice these skills on our own so we're more familiar with them in stressful environments and in hard conversations that feel like they may lead to greater conflict. Practice staying *in* your body and accessing safety inside yourself–this helps determine whether we should stay and participate or leave until all parties feel more ready to engage.

RADICAL ACCEPTANCE

We're all going to get it wrong sometimes. Even when we have the best of intentions, there is no way to be a perfect human—in fact, being human is

HARD. Practice the radical acceptance of doing the best we can while wanting to still learn better. Let's hold ourselves accountable, pivot with ownership and compassion when we get it wrong and risk bigger for a safer, more vibrant world. Let's each do our part, as messy and awkward as it will be, let's lean into it because people matter, a safer world matters—you matter.

Henry recently came into the office with a pep in his step, plunking down on the couch and smiling. I've come to recognize his expressions and knew this one likely meant he had something exciting to share.
"I did it—I got mad without either of us feeling scared."

I'm smiling now too, picturing how moments like these call for a dousing of confetti—I still haven't found a way to do it in my office that doesn't involve a mess to clean up but I intend to find one! I nod my head and lean forward, encouraging him to share, anticipating the new ground he's taking. "Say more Henry."

"You know it's been hard—ever since she found out about the affair I've felt so ashamed. All I used to want to do was push back when she'd bring it up. But, you know, we've been practicing talking about what I've been working on in therapy and I told her about our last session, the one where we explored how I betrayed myself before I betrayed her. She was upset because she didn't feel validated and went in for a low dig.

I felt it—I felt that wave of rage, felt that part of me that sounds just like my fucking dad. That energy showed up and I wanted to just shut her up, but then—MEL—I took a breath instead and then another one and another. I could feel it all organizing inside me. I looked at her and instead of feeling angry I felt ...so sorry instead. I'd hurt her...I was such a dick. I told her too—and it was then that I finally realized it. I'M NOT MY DAD. I'm me. I can be angry and wrong without blowing shit up."

The grin on his face is unmatchable—Henry and I are both somewhere between a laugh and a sob, my heart is nearly exploding with his as he describes being able to stay in his body, his breath, care for his partner's wound more softly, see himself more clearly. He is not his dad.

A House Restored

He knows this *because* he's learning how to practice embodiment, which in turns means he can be with his anger differently. Instead of becoming flooded by emotions he's learning how to cope with them, welcoming his wounded childhood memories and experiences home and choosing to gentleness with himself instead. In essence, he can now hold a bomb because he knows how to dismantle it—there is no threat.

I want this for you.

This freedom, healing and safety is meant for *you* too! Learning how to be with our feelings and stay in our bodies empowers us to access internal consent, practice it more fully with others and build a safer world for future generations to be born into.

Becoming *homebodied* is a way we *live* as ourselves in the company of others, how we reclaim what's broken, redeem what's been discarded, build an altar as a lighthouse for every prodigal part to find their way home.

Lest we forget: *life is for the living.*

every day I send a love note
light is fading, head home darling
before it's dark, the sky is falling
head home now, to yourself

may you let love gather 'round
your recovering heart
your good, good body
may every part kneel in safe surrender
near the hearth inside you

may you notice how
the warmth of your fire
opens doors
how every room inside you
is touched by the light

Chapter Nine

HOMECOMING

On a walk with the puppy, I pass a house with several flags and political signs, one of which reads "If you keep voting Democrat you're going to kill America' and for more than one reason my face flinches—the rhetoric feels extreme, the language violent. I can't help but consider the duality of the framework and the assumptions made regarding what 'America' and 'Democrat' even mean—also the juxtaposition of identifying and voting one way and having only a singular outcome. A wave of discouragement rides through me, the sign feels lacking in the complexity and nuance consent and personhood deserve.

Don't fret—this isn't a sneaky, little section I squeezed in to try and influence anyone in a particular political way. I rarely identify with the dominant systems of power and identity that white supremacy has built, which includes mainstream political parties. This reflection is more or less an observation of how now when I experience any one of us reduced to having a singular option I pause, sift, and try to invite more curiosity around why I feel what I feel, why my face grimaces the way she does.

I do this walk regularly when the weather here in the desert permits, often finding movement stimulates the places I feel bound by an emotion or stuck with an unfinished thought. Tonight I'm reflecting on a current situation I've had difficulty honoring boundaries with. For all the encouragement this book intends to provide, I *do* get how consent can be difficult to access, boundaries are often excruciating to set and maintain. They can also be challenging to honor when others set them *for us*.

This last year I grieved the loss of a close friendship. While it may evolve into something else in a different season, for now I've been invited to accept where it's at and the boundaries this person has set with me. It's one of only a handful of relationships I've grieved this hard, and, if I'm truly honest with myself, I have not been as gracious as I'd hoped to be with letting go.

My friend asked for space, and twice over the months that followed the request I still sent a message, checking in without overt expectations, letting them know I was thinking of them, communicated that I was not expecting nor entitled to a response. I can see now how the underbelly of that energy was wrapped up and tangled inside my pain and longing for reconnection. I genuinely didn't want them to write back if it wasn't in alignment, yet can now see how neither message honored the boundary for space this friend had asked me for. Both attempts, despite my best intentions, were violations of the limit they'd set. I grieve that now just as I grieve the loss of our friendship. I wish I'd honored their consent and request for space differently. They deserve that—we all deserve that.

I bring this up now, vulnerable as it is, because I want to validate how even when we know better, we don't always show up as we ought to and it causes harm. It can feel tender, challenging and all levels of inner-earth-quaking to honor another person's '*yes, no and maybe*'. It's also hard when we set a boundary with someone we value and they continue trespassing it and we have to draw firmer lines as a result. As much as I'm grieving the loss of this friendship, I want my friend to maintain their boundary believing it's what serves their needs for safety. Healing from trauma and grief often means reckoning with pain caused *to us*, the losses we've incurred—it also includes reckoning with the pain *we've* caused others. From my experience it's always been both.

It feels important to continue reflecting this reality: I am in the messiness with you. We are reclaiming our paths together, learning embodiment together, rebuilding a safer world together–I *get* it's unfamiliar and tender, nonetheless, I implore us to take further ground and ownership still. I want to be someone I trust to honor the boundaries set for me, want to look at myself clearly, deepen into the kind of person who is determined to stay in alignment with my values, resetting as many times as my integrity convicts me to.

I want this for you too, believing it's possible for us to grow into safety for ourselves and communities. It remains important to own and practice transparency with where and how we fall short. There are many layers to this book that feel unresolved for me, yet I've determined to include them because I believe that the third-way, messy middle, awkward growth of reclaiming ourselves is worth the risk. I want as many people as possible healing and becoming more free.

I'm willing to experience criticism for where and how I got things wrong if there's a chance that one person ends up feeling more safe. You are worth that risk.

I'm anchored to a hope bigger than my own path—my integrity is anchored to my core, she keeps calling me to hard lines and the parts of myself worth looking more honestly at. Embodied consent remains an invitation worthy of experimentation and perhaps some social disruption—we can create a safer world.

Multiple times throughout writing this book I stalled, the work either temporarily unclear or overwhelming. My editor Megan would kindly, assertively say some variation of the following, "*Your writing is going to trigger you—there is no way around that, and, if you are willing to be honest in your writing, it's going to trigger others as well.*"

What we didn't talk about then but have since talked through, is that while my writing *did* at times trigger me, naming and owning my story healed me too. Leaning in has reunited more of me with my body. It bears repeating: I believe this for you too.

A while back I took a barre class after a several-years-long sabbatical from the gym (*ahem*) or at least that's how I'm referring to it. My friend Michele and I were *so* sore the next day, even my neck muscles hurt! There was a particular moment at the end of class that caught me off guard—the instructor had put on a slower song for the cooldown, the beat and lyrics began reverberating in my chest cavity. My breath slowed as I felt the familiarity of a melody that in a previous life I might've heard played during communion back when I attended church. The words were an invitation to be radically loved where we are, as we are—lyrics describing a love I had craved yet only experienced as fragmented due to the many conditions and caveats it was offered alongside.

I stretched into an extended triangle pose, my fingers stretching upward towards the light filtering through the room. As I leaned into the stretch the lyrics settled within me, a thought surfacing that surprised me, genuinely catching me off guard: I miss God.

I exhaled and drew that thought in, at first sharply, later with curiosity. I don't actually miss the god of my childhood. Dr. Christena Cleveland, theologian and social psychologist, introduced me years ago to the terminology of *'white, male god'* to describe the one constructed and upheld in western, evangelical Christianity.

It is 'that god' Dr. Cleavland describes that is most reflected throughout my childhood and lived experience. I could never go back to him—let me be clear: *I would never choose him.*

I continued to hold the longing that surfaced in that barre class with curiosity though, realizing perhaps I had other choices. I had been following my own spiritual path since leaving religion, connecting to the Divine and source through other avenues—nature, spirit, humans, science, astrology, art. I already feel connected to my spirituality, so why the "I miss God" thought?

Like other areas in my life, my freedom and alignment had come from giving myself more options. I needed permission to leave my marriage in order to have permission to stay married, needed permission to leave motherhood so that I could energetically choose to parent, honoring my children from a deeper place than obligation had offered me. I trust my integrity deeply, knowing that when I connect to my inner compass and have freedom to choose, I imperfectly yet consistently choose what's in alignment with who I want to be and consequently, also ends up being what's safer and kinder for those around me.

It'd been different with the god I grew up with though–I needed permission to leave him in order to heal, no one gave me permission to leave but me—once I felt permission to choose I discerned I had to leave, had to outright *lose him* in order to save my life. I could not choose us both. Christianity was for me, a transactional relationship based on my self- betrayal.

It was clear for me then and remains clear now—there would have been no way to stay and live in embodied, wholehearted alignment. White, male god demanded an abandonment of myself and a participation in harm towards others. I do not regret losing him nor do I question my decision to stay away.

"I miss God."

The words echoed inside me nonetheless, as I practiced curiosity those words eventually expanded into a deeper revelation as I held the longing inside my opening body: *What if I healed God inside of me?* What if by doing so I could choose their return—what if God was mine to reclaim on my terms, like every other part of my story and body's history?

Tears sprang to my eyes as I considered how, even now, I am allowed to choose a different God–*how I'm allowed to love God,* allowed to outline what I will yield and subsequently also refuse—if I lost God before I could lose another God again.

What if, I could love and be loved by the God of my own longing?

In the same ways that the expression of choosing marriage and parenthood seemingly appeared similar on the surface despite following a deep-earth-quaking-energetic-shift, I imagine my choosing of God will too. That's the irony: I became free by shedding an old framework no one else measured although those closest to me softly felt. I am my own witness and governess, what if you are too?

I've said this before and may say it forevermore: I am less invested in what and whom you choose, less invested in where you reclaim and how you root. Whether you are polyamorous, monogamous, religious or childless—whether you love being a parent, punch a clock, sometimes leave your body, farm the land, or none of the above and still don't give a fuck—*I am invested in you being you.*

Mel Gentry Bosna

Invested, in you becoming the most awake, alive version of yourself you've ever been. Invested in you living freely and wholly in the home of your body—the results being clearer alignment with your integrity, intuition and sovereignty.

I trust where you root when you journey towards that earth is through embodied consent and self-accountability.

Perhaps our lives become a collection of milestones that willingly terraform into a walkable path. When laid together they might create that messy-middle-third-way-path which has the creativity and audacity to point us towards our homecoming. Even then—*even then*—we get to choose where and when we follow.

Pavers come in all shapes, sizes and seasons, much like people. Yours could manifest as one of the many that follow: resigning from a toxic job, eating an 'unsafe; food, signing divorce papers, attending a meeting for the first or the 293rd time, twirling in your first skirt, cutting your hair or perhaps, leaving the church. You might've sent capitalism a middle finger and chosen to rest—or maybe, *just maybe*, it's the decision you made, following that pregnancy test.

I see you and am with you, my hands are decidedly here at your back. There is no 'right' way to be human, there is however, a way to return home to save *you*.

No one persons' map nor directions will be identical. I beg you to notice the spaces where your smallness is not required, where your whispers are amplified so others hear and know you. The places where we're all welcome at the table with the understanding that weapons must be left at the door. Notice how your body feels as you lean into this expansive understanding—you are as big as the ocean, as wholly restored as you forgive and repair your ache to be.

If you risk more you will undoubtedly get much wrong and remain a growing, awkward-kind-of-human—*my favorite kind*.

I'll adore you all the more for the vulnerability of showing up and leaning into the goal of repairing instead of avoiding or perfecting. I want more for you and believe it is possible, even now. *Nothing*, I mean it—nothing negates it as an option moving forward. You are allowed to choose a new way as often as needed. You can and must save your life. May you never cease hearing the call to head back to your body and story.

A House Restored

I trust the good inside you, so go ahead, *head home.*

Your body is waiting, head home, head home, run and return, stake claim to every nook and corner of your belonging. The fire is burning, the table has been set, the light is filtering through.

The world will be safer for it. You are a life worth saving, I promise and mean it—you are worth coming home to. In the meantime should you forget, you are not alone on this journey nor will you be in your homecoming.

Appendix

Acknowledgments

To my friends, whose faithful hands remain steady at my back–you are my daily bread and water and undoubtedly the greatest love affairs of my life: Crystal, Bethany, Sarah, Jess, Christine, Kimberly, Jami, Venessa and Steph. You are deep wells of love, thank you for being trustworthy.

To my parents–you've shown me the ways in which people fall in and out and back in love again. Thank you for loving others wholeheartedly and for your willingness to show up now when I need you. In this way I hope to be just like you.

A million waves of gratitude to Michael and Annie Kassenbrock. I found an alternative way in this great big world because you saw fit to clear a path for my education. Much of who I've become is due to your investment: you homed me and claimed me as family. I will never, *not ever* stop longing for one more hug and conversation with Michael and Travis. I hope they're proud of me. Annie, Dylan, Logan and Coleman–I'm glad for you.

Livia and Locke, I've been and remain a very human mother, it's an honor to be yours. May you discover the way home to yourselves should you lose it, may you feel how very, very glad I am that you are you and not anyone else. I hope you listen to your inner compass and honor your inner *'yes, no and maybe.'*

Andy, regardless of where the road goes I can write with precious clarity and deepening gratitude how proud I am of us. Twenty years in and we're still discovering how to choose ourselves which is allowing us to choose our relationship from a different energy. May we continue taking risks on behalf of a vibrant life.

To those who participated in the research as a client, interview participant, sounding board, administrative assistant or editor–THANK YOU. Your stories

Acknowledgements

are precious and I did my best to honor the fullness of your humanity. Thank you for sharing yourself so generously with this project, your fingerprints are all over the safer world we're co-creating.

Jennie Kerns, Nina Love, Karley Ghaby and Megan February—I couldn't have created this book without your practical support, expansive wisdom and badass skills. You're the best and this book is all the better for it. Gail Henderson, Venessa De la Cruz, Chidimma Ozor Commer and Kimberly Deckel—your feedback on the systems that hijack consent with specificity to white body supremacy was worth immeasurably more than can be quantified or compensated. Thank you for your willingness to call me in, both my integrity and this book are clearer as a result.

Malialani Dullanty, you created the most playful, resonate illustrations and cover art. Commissioning you was admittedly the easiest decision I had with this book. The ways you conceptualized and created the imagery for *The House Of Me* felt like another version of homecoming and your talent seems to have no limits.

It hadn't occurred to me that this big, little book would have a foreword until I met Corinne Shark, then as clearly as it hadn't been a prior consideration it became an unshakable thought. Corinne, I'm equally glad for your audacity to reclaim what many men and systems sought to destroy and for the ways your joy lights a way for others to do so to. Thank you for writing me one hell of an epitaph—*ahem*, I mean foreword.

Lastly, an abundance of confetti-bull-horn-gratitude-energy to my heroes: Kelly Lynn Lunde and Peggy Bilsten. Kelly, you showed the world how to practice radical third-way accountability and I remain in awe. Peggy, the steady rhythm of your power unlocked a key for my own flow. I know the gift of your presence and find it remarkable how I simultaneously felt your hands at my back as often as I experienced you leading the way and clearing a path.

Further Reflection

Journaling Prompts & Book Club Questions

The following section includes questions originally drafted for the qualitative research Mel's team conducted in 2021 and 2022. The set of questions most commonly used in the interviews are italicized, however additional questions are included for further exploration and reflection.

The questions are broken up into three sections, the first of which explores background and childhood development, the second looks at the internal process of your relationship with yourself and the third explores how you practice relationships with others.

They are included here to serve as a guide–whether you use the questions as a journaling prompt, take one as a topic to a therapist or a safe person to explore in conversation or use them in a book club group discussion, my hope is that they lead you further into discovery with yourself. Skip with compassion any question you're not ready to answer and work through answering them at your own pace.

BACKGROUND REFLECTION QUESTIONS

1. Have you sought to mirror the types of intimate relationship/s your caregivers had or have you sought out something different for yourself?

2. Tell me what you remember learning about relationships when you were growing up or alternatively, what do you remember thinking about dating or marriage when you were a child or adolescent?

3. When you were growing up, were you presented with options regarding the types of relationships you could be in? For instance, were same-sex relationships, interracial relationships, being single, getting married/divorced, etc. Were multiple options presented as viable to you?

4. What do you remember learning about consent when you were growing up? If so, what stands out about those experiences?

5. Do you feel like you saw adults model consent or boundaries when you were growing up? What about now?

6. Where did you primarily receive your sexual education? Looking back, do you wish any part of that experience was different?

7. *Are you familiar with purity culture? If so, tell me your thoughts and/or any experience with it that you're comfortable sharing.*

8. Has your definition of consent changed from what you were originally taught? If so, how?

9. Morality is acting in accordance with community/social values, ethics is living inside your own values—what most drives your experience with consent and boundaries?

INTERNAL PROCESS / RELATIONSHIP WITH SELF

1. How would you currently describe your relationship with yourself?

2. What comes to mind when you think of the word embodiment? Is that something you experience ever and if so, how?

3. *How do you know when or how to trust yourself? Can you consent without trusting yourself? How does this feel in your body when you've tried?*

4. How does your body feel or experience things when mentally you are conflicted about giving a 'yes/no' to someone? How do you navigate situations where you're being asked for something and internally you feel conflicted?

5. Can you think about a time when you were certain something (a job, an opportunity, a relationship, a decision, etc.) was either 'right' or 'wrong' for you? If so, how did you know and more importantly, how did your *body* feel? Is that experience of knowing something is 'right' or 'wrong' for you similar or different to how you know you're consenting?

6. *Many of us intellectually know as adults we have more than one option for ourselves—for instance most of us know we could leave a marriage after we've had kids but may not actually feel like we're allowed to because of pressure or fear—do the options you intellectually have match the options you feel like you have?*

7. *Do you give yourself permission to change your mind once you've said yes/no to something? What does that process look like when it happens?*

8. Similar question as to the last, are there times that you do consent and later change your mind or regret it? Or instances where your mind says one thing but your body says another? Tell me as much or little about that process as you're comfortable with.

9. *Do other people's expectations of you confuse whether or not you're saying yes/no or wanted what you agreed to? How can you tell what are your feelings and what's someone else's desire or expectation? Is it always clear or sometimes ambiguous?*

10. Have you ever found yourself abandoning or disconnecting from yourself in order to try and make a relationship work? What does this look or feel like when it's happening?

11. How do you typically handle uncertainty in a relationship?

12. Is there a way you can tell when you're running towards a desire or need versus avoiding/running away from it?

13. *Have you ever felt like you've hidden things from yourself with what you want or need in order to stay in a relationship and/or justify leaving a relationship? If so, what has that experience of self-deception or denial felt like for you?*

14. How can you tell when you're being honest and/or dishonest with yourself?

15. How do you know when you're doing something out of a cultural and/or moral value versus a personal/internal value or ethic?

EXTERNAL PROCESS / RELATIONSHIP WITH OTHERS

1. In what ways do you think consent and boundaries are similar and/or different from each other?

2. What's hard or easy about setting boundaries? (Is it more dependent on what's going on inside of you or consistently the others reaction to your boundary?

3. Once you set a boundary do you feel like you can maintain it? Say more about why or why not.

4. What has your practice with consent or boundaries been like when someone wants something from you that doesn't feel right? How does your body feel when this is happening?

5. *Have you ever been asked about consent outside of a sexual relationship or experience?*

6. Do you find other people and/or family members' expectations influence what you want or say yes/no to? Whose expectations have made knowing what you want the hardest to figure out?

7. Have you ever felt pressured into agreeing to something because you've said yes to it previously? (i.e. volunteering, hanging out with someone, touching someone, etc.)

8. When you're in a relationship, do you find yourself more aware of what you or your partner wants? How can you tell whose desires and needs belong to which one of you—do you experience that in your body?

9. Have the types of relationships you want to be in as an adult evolved in the last 5+ years, and if so, what's contributed to the change?

10. Many people at some point in a relationship find themselves craving something different—whether it's changing the relationship dynamics, boundaries or person/people they're involved with. Lots of things may stop them from expressing their desire, have you had this experience and if so, how have you navigated it?

11. Are your experiences with consent and boundaries similar or different in romantic relationships than your relationships with your family, kids, friends and/or colleagues? Does anything stand out as to why some relationships are easier to consent to and others harder?

12. Do you feel like one person's "yes/no" is more meaningful than yours in a relationship? What contributes to that "yes/no" response you just gave?

13. What have you experienced as the lessons men and women learn from bad relationships or bad sex—do you feel these lessons have been similar or different than yours and/or your partners?

14. How do you know whether or not the type of relationship you're in is in alignment or "right" for you?

15. How do you know whether or not monogamy, ethical non-monogamy, singleness, polyamory, divorce, etc. is in alignment or "right" for you?

16. Have you felt like you need to keep parts of yourself hidden or locked away in order to be in a relationship with people you care about? If so, how has this impacted you? How has it impacted the relationship over time?

17. Do you feel like your family is supportive and safe enough for you to explore the type of intimate relationship you desire being in?

18. *Have you ever abandoned your boundaries or values in a last ditch effort to save a relationship? (Any type of relationship) If you answered yes, what do you observe about this pattern now?*

19. Does your cultural and/or religious identification create more or less safety for you to explore what feels in alignment with yourself? Does it ever block you from consenting to your own desires or obligate you into pleasing others?

20. Can you consent without trusting the other person you're in relationship with? Have you ever tried?

How To Choose A Therapist

I often tell people that picking a therapist is a bit like dating–a weird metaphor I know. In the same way I wouldn't presume all people would want to date me (I'm well aware they don't, ha!), I don't presume I'll be a great clinical fit for all people seeking out a therapist. Any clinician who takes it personally when they are not a good fit for their client is, from my perspective, exhibiting a bright, red flag of immaturity or narcissism.

Every one of us brings ourselves to relationship: healed, wounded, exiled and reclaimed parts are present in the room whether we're aware of them or not. To assume a clinician is any less human than their clients is an act of dishonesty and what I believe contributes to greater issues of transference and countertransference for both the client and therapist.

Clinical ethics dictate clear boundaries surrounding therapeutic relationships– they are not mutually reciprocal, meaning that the therapist's needs, shared experiences, feelings and triggers are not for the client to care for or support— while a therapist's personal disclosure *can* be therapeutically appropriate and trust-building at times it requires discernment, self-awareness and accountability for a therapist to understand the reasons for disclosure and how it may impact clients. Any clinician believing they are above causing clients harm is negligent and dangerous.

Trauma is a word that's used more often now and if you're searching for a therapist you might see it commonly identified as a specialty. I'd encourage you to ask a clinician what their training and approach is with trauma work and how it's evolved.

While all mental health providers are governed by a code of ethics and state and national boards that enforce them, not all therapists are trained equally nor do they share the same specialties, approaches and values. I ask my clients to pay attention to how their body feels in my office space, how they feel coming to therapy and also after they leave. I also encourage my clients to pay attention to how they feel when interacting with me, knowing that even if I'm intentionally asking that they may not be fully comfortable sharing with me in the moment given the power dynamic that therapy presents.

My hope is that clients experience a safe enough space to feel seen and cared for as they are, supported with becoming more of who they want to be, challenged in ways that honor their limits and consent, validated where they've experienced harm and invited into deeper ownership regarding where they themselves caused harm. Seeing as how I too am human and am not above harm, I seek to practice repair with my clients and myself if or when there's a breach of trust or misunderstanding.

(POTENTIAL) QUESTIONS TO ASK A MENTAL HEALTH PROVIDER

A new client recently asked during her intake appointment how I practice care and boundaries so I don't take home all the stress from my work–I smiled, loving that she asked that question and understood the importance of boundaries to avoid compassion fatigue and burn-out. Nobody is above this vulnerability so stewarding it is crucial–the following are examples of questions that you might consider asking a clinician to get a sense for fit and experience.

Mind you, I am NOT suggesting you copy and paste these in an email when you send an inquiry! More or less that you feel free to include them in your interactions with a clinician and discern what feels in alignment with the information you're seeking to determine fit.

There aren't right or wrong responses so to speak, however if you're paying attention to your own body and energy and note the posture and energy of the clinician's response I believe you'll be able to discern what you need to regarding whether they feel like a good fit for you.

1. Are you willing to share why you chose this as a career and how it's similar or different from why you're still doing it?

2. How do you see your role as a therapist?

3. What are ways you hold yourself accountable and/or practice humility with this role?

4. What is your approach to trauma work? How can you tell if a client is ready?

5. What are ways you practice boundaries or self-care so that you have something to offer clients?

6. Can you tell me more about _____ specialty or modality? I've heard of it but don't really know what it means.

7. How do you tell if a client isn't a good fit for you? How do you determine you're not a good fit for a client? What do you do when that's the case?

8. How will I know if this is a fit and/or if I'm making progress in therapy?

9. How long do clients typically work with you?

10. What is your perspective on how people heal?

While the mental health field is rapidly evolving as are the methods utilized for treating the holistic needs of clients, I defer to modalities that prioritize somatic treatment (body based) and are built on a foundation and practice of consent. Examples currently include: Internal Family Systems/Parts work (IFS), Somatic Experience (SE), Brain-Spotting and at times EMDR when paired with an aforementioned modality and clinician who still centers embodiment.

Sources & Works Consulted

Key Terms

Menakem, R. (2017). *My Grandmother's Hands: Racialized Trauma and the Pathway to Mending Our Hearts and Bodies.* Central Recovery Press.

Chapter One

Burke, T. (2021). *Unbound, My Story of Liberation and the Birth of the Me Too Movement.* Flatiron Books: An Oprah Book.

Van Der Kolk, B. (2014). *The Body Keeps the Score: Brain, Mind, and Body in the Healing of Trauma.* Penguin Publishing Group

Chapter Two

Febos, M. (2022). *Body Work: The Radical Power of Personal Narrative.* Catapult.

Chapter Three

Nagoski, E., Nagoski, A. (2020). *Burnout: The Secret to Unlocking the Stress Cycle.* Random House Publishing.

Febos, M. (2019). *Girlhood.* Bloomsbury Publishing.

Sources & Works Consulted

Chapter Four

McBride, H. (2021). *The Wisdom of Your Body*. Brazos Press.

Chapter Five

Allison, E.J. (2022). *#ChurchToo: How Purity Culture Upholds Abuse and How to Find Healing*. Broadleaf Books. hooks, b. (2010). *Understanding Patriarchy.* Louisville Anarchist Federalist

Baldoni, J, Plank L, & Heath, J. (Hosts). (2021, July 26). Alok Vaid-Menon: The Urgent Need for Compassion. [Audio Podcast Episode]. In The Man Enough Podcast. Wayfarer Studios, P&G Studios, in Partnership with Cadence 13. http://manenough.com/alok/

Channing Brown, A. (2018). *I'm Still Here: Black Dignity in a World Made for Whiteness.* Convergent Books.

Friedman, J. & Valenti, J. (2019). *Yes Means Yes: Visions of Female Sexual Power and a World Without Rape.* Seal Press.

Greene, S. (2023). *In the Direction of You.*

Henry, A. (2022). *All the White Friends I Couldn't Keep: Hope—and Hard Pills to Swallow—About Fighting for Black Lives.* Convergent Books.

Kendall, M. (2021). *Hood Feminism: Notes from the Women that a Movement Forgot.* Penguin Books.

Lewis Herman, J. (2015). *Trauma and Recovery: The Aftermath of Violence-- From Domestic Abuse to Political Terror*. Basic Books.

Lorde, A. (2007) *Sister Outsider*. Crossing Press.

Menakem, R. (2022) *The Quaking of America: An Embodied Guide to Navigating Our Nation's Upheaval and Racial Reckoning.* Central Recovery Press.

Saad, L. F. (2020) *Me & White Supremacy: Combat Racism, Change the World, and Become a Good Ancestor*. Sourcebooks.

Zahm, M. (2022) If It's Not God [Song].

Chapter Six

Bell, R. (Host). 2017, Feb. The Thing in the Air: Part 1—Our Body. [Audio Podcast Episodes 138, 139, 141, & 142]. In *The RobCast*. *https://robbell.com/podcast/all-episodes/*

Chapter Seven

Blair, G. (2022) *Ejaculate Responsibly: A Whole New Way To Think About Abortion*. Workman Publishing Company.

McKowen, L. (2020). *We are the Luckiest: The Surprising Magic of a Sober Life*. New World Library.

Neff, K. (2015) *Self-Compassion: The Proven Science of Being Kind to Yourself.* William Morrow Paperbacks.

Chapter Eight

Schwartz, R. (2021). *No Bad Parts: Healing Trauma and Restoring Wholeness with Internal Family Systems*. Sounds True.

About the Author

Melodee Gentry Bosna (she/her) has a BS in Sociology and Masters of Social Work and is licensed as a clinical social worker in Arizona where she runs a private practice. She's more commonly known as 'Mel Gentry Bosna' by those who've met her, passionate about joining people on their reclamation journey and aims to agitate systems of oppression (side-eyeing you capitalism, white supremacy, patriarchy and ableism). Her love of the desert, fizzy beverages and stinky cheeses borders on problematic. Mel identifies as a cis-woman, clinician, writer and mother, most of all, she identifies as human.